a slice of the good life

EDITOR-IN-CHIEF
SHEHERAZADE GOLDSMITH

DK

LONDON, NEW YORK,
MUNICH, MELBOURNE, DELHI

Project Editor Susannah Steel
Editor Zia Allaway
Project Designer Claire Legemah
Photography Peter Anderson
Main Contributor Anne Gatti
Contributors Daphne Lambert,
Erica Bower, Pat Thomas,
Matilda Lee, Rob Yarham
Managing Editor Anna Kruger
Managing Art Editor Alison Donovan
DTP Designer Louise Waller
Picture Research Lucy Claxton,
Mel Watson
Production Controller Rebecca Short

Previously published as
A Slice of Organic Life
in Great Britain in 2007
by Dorling Kindersley Ltd
80 Strand London WC2R 0RL

First paperback edition published in
2010 by Dorling Kindersley Limited

A Penguin Company

2 4 6 8 10 9 7 5 3 1

A CIP catalogue record for this book is
available from the British Library.

ISBN 978-1-4053-5341-0

Reproduced by
Wyndehams-Icon, London
Printed and bound by
Sheck Wah Tong, China

Discover more at
www.dk.com

a slice of the good life

CONTENTS

2 ROOF TERRACE, PATIO OR TINY GARDEN

3 GARDEN, ALLOTMENT OR FIELD

INTRODUCTION

Until a few years ago, individuals who were concerned about the state of the environment were considered alarmist. The only people really involved in any kind of campaigning were environmentalists, who have long appeared to non-environmentalists as slightly eccentric. How could something as rich and vast as the planet be affected by our lifestyles? The possibility that we might actually be exhausting its resources was inconceivable then.

Now that is changing, and fast. You can't open a newspaper without being made aware of the impact of our lives on the planet... the extinction of species, melting glaciers, freak weather events, water shortages and so on, each more horrifying than the next. We now know from endless scientific studies that we are actively destroying the only planet we know that can sustain us. Indeed, if everyone in the world lived the life of the average person in the UK, we would need three planets of identical natural resources in order to sustain us.

Until I became a mother, I was as relaxed as the next person about the state of the natural world. I was aware of the issues, but I rarely lost sleep over them, and if something grabbed my attention, I was usually able to push it to one side believing there was no point worrying – and that, in any case, the world is full of professional people devoted to tackling these trends. But worrying is what mothers do best, and with three small children of my own, stories about rising sea levels, pesticide residues on our foods, and the increase of childhood cancers were no longer so abstract. I soon began to question my own way of life and became aware of the need to find alternatives to my existing habits.

The Iroquois people of North America demanded of their elders that they take decisions only after considering the impact it would have on the seventh generation yet to come. It seems to me that this is exactly the approach we badly need. Without it, the kind of world we might end up passing on to our grandchildren doesn't bear thinking about.

The effects of our short-sightedness are becoming increasingly obvious, and awareness is now growing. Consumer demand for alternatives has meant that organic food, for instance, has grown from something only lentil munchers eat to mainstream produce. Some of the biggest retailers are even looking into producing organic cotton clothes. There is a race to the top, with some of the world's best-known companies desperately trying to out-green their rivals. The media now feels obliged to cover these issues regularly, and politicians are beginning to act as if being elected depends on environmental leadership.

It's now clear to most people that we need to learn how to live within nature's limits. Even if you're still not fully convinced by the science of climate change, there is, nevertheless, more than enough evidence to justify taking precautions. But knowledge isn't enough, and the risk of doing nothing is too big a price to pay. We need to convert it into action.

We can do an enormous amount simply by changing our daily habits

The good news is that, contrary to what we have often been led to believe, there are many solutions and they don't involve us living deprived and boring lives where our greatest pleasures are forbidden. They are simple, affordable and effortless.

There was a time when recycling presented itself as a chore. Today it's second nature to a growing majority of us. Choosing to buy energy-efficient light bulbs, for example, would lead to dramatic energy savings if we all did it. And if we all choose, wherever possible and within our means, to buy local food that is fresher and healthier for us, we'll be contributing to a reversing decline in our rural communities and helping to reduce emissions resulting from so-called "food miles" (the ingredients in a typical Sunday lunch are likely to have travelled the equivalent of twice around the world before reaching the table, producing 37kg/82lb of carbon dioxide). None of these changes represents a sacrifice.

More importantly, if we shift our lifestyles so that we're living more naturally, a whole world becomes available to us. Nature is generous, clever and beautiful, which is why being in contact with it, whether it be at a food market, in our gardens or planting up a windowbox, brings us great pleasure.

> *Working with nature rather than against it only helps to simplify and enrich our lives*

Changing the way we live can make a significant difference. But the reality is that not everyone will be persuaded. And for many, the initial cost of these changes can make them difficult to undertake, which is why it is important to campaign to make the alternatives accessible. It's amazing what a small, but focused campaign can achieve. We need to let our local MPs and decision-makers know that we are aware of the facts, and the alternatives. For instance, it's obvious to many of us that an apple that has been sprayed with several chemicals to keep it fresh and then flown halfway across the world to be sold should be more expensive that one grown organically in our country and transported from a few hundred kilometres away. And yet it's not.

If the true costs of large-scale modern farming appeared on the price tag of "cheap" food, it wouldn't be anything like as cheap. In the UK, for example, £250 million of taxpayers' money is used to extract pesticides from water supplies each year. So consumers, in effect, pay twice – over the counter and through their taxes.

I hope that what this book will show is that the joys of eating seasonally, growing your own food, keeping bees, making compost or keeping chickens are real, that being more conscientious isn't about giving up things. On the contrary, it's about rediscovering the simple pleasures of life. How can throwing a ready-made meal into the microwave compare with the satisfaction of preparing a meal made with real organic, even home-grown, ingredients (be they herbs or pork)?

Each chapter provides simple ideas and examples of how we can lessen our impact on the world and improve the quality of our lives. Some of the topics may at first seem insignificant, but it's impossible to exaggerate the value of acting together. We all need to eat, for instance, and so the tiniest change in the way we eat has profound and wide-ranging implications. The hardest part is altering our daily habits.

It's impossible to exaggerate the value of acting together

Each of us has a role to play in reversing the decline of our planet, whether it's turning our televisions off at the socket or installing a wood-burning stove. I'm certain that knowing you're part of the solution and not the problem is good for the soul. And with every passing day, our chances of reversing the damage to the planet increase as the number of people willing to take a stand grows. It's finally possible to be optimistic.

S. Goldsmith

1 NO NEED FOR A GARDEN

GROW SALAD LEAVES IN A WINDOWBOX

Baby leaf salads are a gourmet treat when eaten on their own or mixed in with a plain green salad. If you grow your own supply of succulent leaves, you can snip off a handful whenever you want to. All you need is a windowbox, some packets of seeds and potting compost.

Choose a bright window ledge or shelf space for a windowbox, or brackets to sit a windowbox on. The best kind of leaves to grow are cut-and-come-again varieties. These are salads that you eat when the plants are only 5–10cm (2–4in) high, and which will re-sprout so that you can cut them again a few weeks later. You can get up to four cuts from one planting, depending on the kinds you grow. Not only are these baby leaves really nutritious, they taste sweeter and more succulent than many other types, and are ready to be harvested as early as three weeks after sowing. Because the leaves are picked when the plant is young they can be grown really close together, so you will get an impressive quantity of leaves, even from a small windowbox.

Prepare your windowbox

The larger and longer the box, the less likely it is to dry out. To give the plants the best chance to grow, it should be at least 20cm (8in) wide and 15cm (6in) deep, and should have several drainage holes. It needs to be positioned in a sunny or lightly shaded spot. A plastic box is lighter and easier to move, but if you use a wooden or clay box, make sure the ledge is sturdy enough to take the weight of it when full. Sitting the box on a drainage tray helps to keep moisture in and prevents water splashing down the wall or over the ledge.

Grow salad leaves

Salad leaves need rich, well-drained soil and constant moisture. Put a layer of crocks or pebbles in the base of the windowbox and fill it with good-quality, multi-purpose compost. Moisten the soil and sow seeds thinly, covering them lightly with compost, from early spring onwards. Once germinated, thin the seedlings. If you go away, ask a friend to water, or set up a self-watering system, such as an upturned plastic bottle with the bottom cut off and small holes drilled close to the cap – fill the bottle and the water will slowly drip through the holes. Stick copper tape around the windowbox to keep slugs and snails out. When they are finger height, cut the leaves about 3cm (1¼in) above the soil and leave to re-grow.

For salad mixes, thin the seedlings to 3cm (1¼in) apart.

For rocket, thin the seedlings to around 15cm (6in) apart.

For loose-leaf lettuces Sow the seeds in a pot or module indoors in early spring and then transfer the seedlings to the windowbox after the frosts, spacing them about 20cm (8in) apart.

Salad mixes

If you like a variety of flavours, try one of the salad mixes offered by seed companies. These are normally selected to blend well together – for example, spicy or oriental leaves such as mizuna, French and Italian – and to be ready for cutting at about the same time. Some include soft-leaved herbs such as chervil and basil. Salad rocket, which has a delicious peppery taste, grows particularly fast and can bolt (race to the flowering stage) in hot weather. If you have room for another windowbox or pot, it's worth growing salad rocket on its own. Try sowing it a bit later to pick in autumn and winter when your other salad has stopped growing. You could also grow loose-leaf lettuces, such as 'Salad Bowl', 'Lollo Rossa' and 'Catalogna' types, which you can harvest when the plants are 10–15cm (4–6in) high. In a 60cm (24in) windowbox you could raise three plants, and if you choose three different varieties you should get enough leaves to make delicious mixed salads throughout the summer.

Winter salads

You can even grow a crop of salad leaves in winter by starting them off indoors in modules and hardening them off (putting them outside during the day, but bringing them indoors at night until they become used to the colder temperatures) before planting out into the windowbox. In frosty weather, the crop will need to be protected with horticultural fleece or a cloche. Good choices to try are winter purslane, mizuna, salad rocket and corn salad.

Choose your salad leaves

Home-grown leaves taste fresher and sweeter than pre-packed portions. They will grow all year, although winter growth is slower.

Summer varieties

Loose-leaf lettuce types (*Latuca sativa*) such as:

- 'Salad Bowl'
- 'Lollo Rossa'
- 'Catalogna'
- 'Bijou'
- 'Bionda a Foglia 'Riccia'
- 'Oak Leaf'
- Oriental mustards (*Brassica juncea*) such as 'Giant Red'
- 'Golden Streaks'
- Salad rocket (*Eruca sativa*)
- Mizuna (*Brassica rapa*)
- Corn salad aka lamb's lettuce (*Valerianella locusta*)

Winter varieties

- Winter purslane aka claytonia (*Montia perfoliata* or *Claytonia perfoliata*)
- Mizuna (*Brassica rapa*)
- Salad rocket (*Eruca sativa*)
- Corn salad aka lamb's lettuce (*Valerianella locusta*)
- Land cress aka American land cress (*Barberea verna*)
- Oriental mustard (*Brassica juncea*) 'Green-in-Snow'

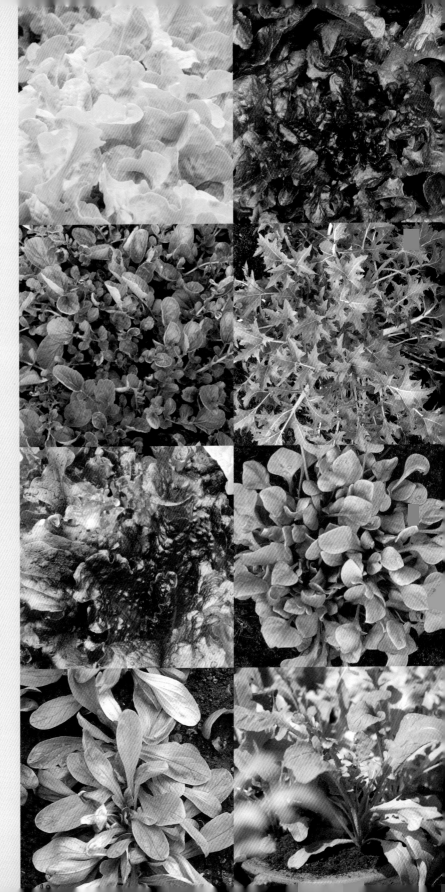

SAVE ENERGY THE EASY WAY

Why save energy? Most domestic energy supplies use fossil fuels (oil, coal and gas), but burning these to create power produces carbon dioxide – one of the main greenhouse gases. So, by saving energy in our homes, we can help to minimize climate change.

Saving energy is easy. It can involve as little as turning off a light switch, to investing in house insulation and energy-efficient appliances. Since we pay for every unit of energy we use, saving energy also saves money.

Simple home improvements

Around 40 per cent of the heat in a typical home is lost through the walls and the roof, so make sure that yours are insulated, if possible. Loft insulation is quick to install and reduces heating bills – the greenest type available is made

from sheep's fleece. Fitting an insulating jacket around your hot water tank will also help, or think about upgrading to a condensing boiler that can save a third on your heating bills.

Turn off any lights you are not using. It is a myth that leaving lights on uses less energy than "warming them up" and this is not true for any modern bulbs. Energy-efficient light bulbs use about a quarter of the electricity and last eight times longer than conventional bulbs.

Buy energy-efficient household appliances: by changing to more efficient models of washing machines, fridges and dishwashers, you can save up to 33 per cent every year on electricity bills. White goods now come with a rating from A to G, A being the most efficient model, so look for the symbol when you buy an appliance.

Small changes that make a big difference

■ Turn off the TV and other appliances left on standby mode and unplug mobile phone chargers: eight per cent of electricity used at home is wasted by equipment on standby.

■ Put lids on your pans while you are cooking and choose the right size pans for the cooker rings. Heating beyond the pan edge just warms air and wastes energy.

■ Use the washing machine only when you have a full load. Washing at 40°C (104°F) instead of 60°C (140°F) uses a third less electricity.

■ Close your curtains in winter to keep out cold draughts.

■ Dry clothes outside on a sunny day, rather than using the tumble dryer.

■ Don't overfill the kettle; boil the amount of water you need.

■ Turn the temperature thermostat down by 1°C (2°F) to reduce your heating consumption by about ten per cent.

■ Nearly 70 per cent of the energy we use in our homes is used for heating rooms. Check that your boiler is running efficiently and have it serviced once a year.

■ Keep your fridge running efficiently by cleaning dust off the condenser coils at the back of it. Dirty coils use up to 30 per cent more energy.

■ If your freezer isn't full, fill the spaces with crumpled newspaper to keep it running as efficiently as possible.

■ Sign up with a green electricity supplier.

Energy facts

● Increasingly high levels of greenhouse gases are trapping heat in the atmosphere that would otherwise escape into space. This extra heat is causing the world's climates to change. Energy efficiency is the quickest, cheapest and cleanest way to reduce greenhouse gas emissions, and to extend the world's energy supplies.

● When you turn on an ordinary incandescent light bulb, only 10% of the electricity used is turned into light. The other 90% is wasted as heat.

● One energy-efficient light bulb will save up to £7 and around 40kg (88lb) of CO_2 every year.

● If every household in the UK changed to energy-efficient light bulbs, enough energy would be saved to power the lighting in two million homes for a year.

● You can calculate how much energy your household uses (your "carbon footprint") at various websites.

SHOP ETHICALLY

Every purchase you make has either a direct or an indirect effect on your own health, on human and animal welfare and on the environment. By asking yourself a few questions before you buy anything, you can effectively improve all of these situations and know that your impact on the world as a consumer has been a positive one. Ultimately, this way of shopping may also help you to improve your own quality of life.

Before making a purchase, ask yourself the following questions:

- Where has the item come from?
- How and who made the product? Were they treated fairly?
- How long will you use the item for, and then can you recycle it? Or will it simply end up sitting in a landfill site for the next century or so?
- How many miles has it had to travel before reaching you? Is there a less polluting alternative?
- Is it truly fresh? What is keeping it looking so fresh?

Changing the way you shop could not be easier, as there are plenty of interesting and enjoyable ways of doing it.

Check out the label Don't trust a label just because the word "fresh" has been written in bright, bold letters across the product, for example. Find out more about what each labelling scheme is actually regulating, and then make your choice accordingly.

Buy organic Farmers registered as organic producers are allowed to use just seven natural pesticides on a restricted basis, as opposed to commercial farmers who can use up to 450 pesticides. It is now generally acknowledged that these large combinations of chemicals carry all sorts of health risks, as well as damaging soil structure and wildlife. Different

Unethical practices

- More energy is used in packaging many foods than in the foods themselves.

- The average item on sale in a supermarket has been transported 1,609 km (1,000 miles).

- The distribution of 1kg (2lb 2oz) of apples air-freighted from New Zealand creates its own weight in CO_2 emissions.

- Conventional cotton farming is responsible for 25% of the world's total pesticide use.

- 40% of the non-organic fruit, vegetable and bread samples tested in the UK have been found to contain traces of pesticides.

- 99% of the world's coffee is not fairly traded. Millions of growers still receive less than 1% of the price we pay in shops and coffee bars.

- More than one in four of all fish caught are thrown back dead into the sea – about 27 million tonnes a year.

countries have varying regulations, so it's worth finding out about different regulatory boards and sticking to those that you recognize. Organic food usually tastes much better, too.

Buy seasonal Look out for vegetable box schemes or small producers who advertise on the internet. Buying seasonal food means that you'll be eating the freshest, tastiest fruit and vegetables available; a strawberry eaten in winter never tastes quite as good as one eaten in the summer.

Buy local where possible Find out where your local farm shops and farmers' markets are located. Supporting your own farming industry is crucial to sustaining local communities and reducing food miles. Without our farmers and small independent shops, we won't have such a choice in how we shop or what we eat.

Buy sustainably harvested fish Fish are being removed from the oceans faster than they can reproduce, causing problems for the sea's natural ecosystems. If trends continue, it is estimated that by 2050 we will run out of edible fish. Only buy fish that has been caught by an environmentally responsible fishery, such as those certified by the Marine Stewardship Council (MSC), or that has been farmed organically.

Choose fair trade Fairly traded goods ensure that growers get a fair price for their produce, enabling them to gain economic self-sufficiency and security.

Buy recycled The more demand there is for recycled goods, the more the market will provide them. Look out for recycled options on everyday purchases such as toilet paper, glassware and dustbin liners.

Season	Vegetables in season	Fruit in season
Winter	Beetroot, cabbages, carrots, celeriac, celery, chicory, endive, greens, Jerusalem artichokes, kale, leeks, onions, parsnips, potatoes, pumpkins and squashes, sprouts, swedes, turnips	Pears, rhubarb
Spring	Cabbages, cauliflowers, chicory, greens, leeks, lettuce, purple sprouting broccoli, radishes, watercress	Rhubarb
Summer	Artichokes, asparagus, aubergines, beetroot, broad beans, broccoli, cabbages, carrots, cauliflowers, chard, courgettes, cucumbers, fennel, garlic, green beans, kohlrabi, lettuce, new potatoes, peas, radishes, rocket, spinach, sweetcorn, tomatoes, watercress	Apples, apricots, blackcurrants, blueberries, cherries, gooseberries, loganberries, plums, redcurrants, strawberries, white currants, worcesterberries
Autumn	Beetroot, broccoli, cabbages, carrots, cauliflowers, celeriac, celery, chard, courgettes, fennel, kale, kohlrabi, leeks, onions, peppers and chillies, potatoes, pumpkins and squashes, runner beans, spinach, sweetcorn, tomatoes, turnips	Blackberries, blueberries, raspberries, apples, damsons, pears, plums, greengages

GROW POTS OF HERBS INDOORS

With a sunny windowsill and the right choice of plants, you can create your own mini herb garden indoors and have a constant supply of fresh leaves to flavour your favourite dishes.

Any herb grown indoors needs to be positioned in good natural light. Some herbs, such as basil and thyme, need maximum sunlight and so do best on a south-facing windowsill. Here you could group together individual pots of basil, chives, marjoram, thyme and salad burnet for year-round snipping. Herbs such as parsley and winter savory cope well on cooler windowsills.

Many herbs are easy to grow from seed, although some are tricky to germinate, such as parsley and sage, which are best bought as young plants from a nursery or garden centre (supermarket plants tend to be less robust). You can keep perennial herbs going right through the year by watering and feeding them carefully. Annuals, such as basil, should provide leaves for picking throughout the summer and into autumn. Keep them well-watered, but avoid waterlogging. For a good bushy plant, keep snipping off the growing tips to use in dishes, and don't allow your herbs to flower.

Grow herbs from seed

Seeds need water, light and a constant, minimum temperature (check on the seed packet for details) to germinate. Most are best sown in early spring.

Sow the seeds in seed trays or modules filled with good quality seed compost. Check the seed packets for sowing depths – fine seeds are usually sown on the soil surface, larger ones should be covered with perlite (light natural granules) or compost.

Keep the compost moist, but not wet, and somewhere light and warm, such as on a windowsill or in a propagator with a vented lid. Check the tray regularly as the seeds usually germinate quickly, in 10–14 days.

When the first seedlings appear, turn the tray or propagator around once a day if it is on a windowsill. This prevents the shoots bending towards the light.

Transfer the seedlings to their final pot when they have formed their second set of leaves. Make sure the pot has a drainage hole, add a layer of crocks or pebbles to the bottom, then top up with multi-purpose compost mixed with grit or horticultural sand. If you've used modules, squeeze out each seedling separately, hold it by the leaves and replant in the filled pot. Lever out seedlings from a seed tray with a stick and replant in the same way.

Tips for growing indoor herbs

● To keep the plant compact and encourage new growth, keep picking the leaves.

● Feed plants regularly with liquid plant food, such as seaweed.

● To keep the air humid on hot days, stand herbs with soft leaves on a tray of damp pebbles or spray them with a fine mist of water.

● If your herbs are positioned on a south-facing windowsill, they may need to be shaded from the scorching midday sun.

● Avoid draughts and extremes of temperature.

Herbs for summer
Parsley (*Petroselinum crispum*)

Sweet basil (*Ocimum basilicum*)

Coriander (*Coriandrum sativum*)

Summer savory (*Satureja hortensis*)

Sweet marjoram (*Origanum majorana*)

Salad burnet (*Sanguisorba minor*)

Year-round herbs
Prostrate rosemary (*Rosemarinus officinalis* 'Prostratus' Group)

Wild marjoram (*Origanum vulgare*)

Winter savory (*Satureja montana*)

Mint (*Mentha spicata*)

Sage (*Salvia officinalis*)

Chives (*Allium schoenoprasum*)

Thyme (*Thymus vulgaris*)

Choose your culinary herbs

Pungent herbs, such as marjoram, rosemary, thyme and sage, can add colour and flavour to marinades and dishes as they cook. Delicate flavoured herbs, such as parsley and chives, impart the most flavour and fragrance when sprinkled over hot and cold dishes.

Rosemary
Strong, refreshing taste that gives flavour to meat, fish, bread and oils.

Parsley
Delicate flavour best used uncooked as a garnish sprinkled over dishes.

Thyme
An essential ingredient in bouquet garnis, stews and casseroles. Use sparingly.

Sage
Herb with a distinctive flavour often used in stuffings for pork and chicken.

Chives
Mild herb that is best used uncooked. Sprinkle over salads and soups.

Mint
Fresh, clean tasting herb. Use in drinks and savoury and sweet dishes.

Basil
Spicily fragrant leaves that lift the flavour of sauces, salads and soups.

Wild marjoram
Also known as oregano. Use sparingly in savoury dishes and sauces.

BATHE USING PURE PRODUCTS

A plain vegetable soap is the best way to clean your body, as commercial products – body washes, bath foams and gels and bubble baths – may include harsh detergents that strip the natural protective oils from your skin. But this doesn't mean that bathtime needs to be boring.

You can use any number of delicious organic essential oils to fragrance your bath. To help them disperse in the water, mix four to ten drops of your chosen oil with one tablespoon (15ml/½fl oz) of milk first: the fat in semi-skimmed or whole milk acts as a carrier to help distribute the oils evenly around the bath. For the greatest benefit, choose essential oils that match your skin type *(right)*.

If you want something a little more exotic, consider a fragrant mineral bath. Add a generous handful of Epsom salts and a few drops of your favourite essential oil (mixed with milk, as above) to the water while the bath is running. Epsom salts can be purchased at any chemist for a fraction of the cost of name brand bath salts, which are essentially the same thing. Soaking your body in the salts encourages your skin to release accumulated toxins, and can help relieve tired muscles. So, in addition to being pleasant and safe to use, Epsom salts are therapeutic as well. For a bit of bathtime fizz, add a handful of bicarbonate of soda to the bath at the same time.

Essential oils to match your skin type

Greasy skin
Lavender, orange, lemon, neroli, cypress, ylang-ylang, bergamot.

Normal skin
Palma rosa, geranium, lavender, Roman chamomile, jasmine, neroli, ylang ylang, frankincense, sandalwood, patchouli.

Sensitive skin
Geranium, lavender, German chamomile

Dry or damaged skin
Geranium, lavender, German chamomile, Roman chamomile, clary sage, myrrh.

Stay safe naturally

If you still prefer to buy your bath products, make sure that they are organic. Encourage your local shops to sell safer products and read the label carefully. Avoid any products that contain the following ingredients:

- Sodium lauryl sulphate
- Cocamidopropl betaine
- Colour (indicated by the letters CI, followed by a number)
- Parfum

MAKE FLAVOURED OILS & VINEGARS

Oils and vinegars infused with herbs or fruit add a splash of colour and a burst of flavour to salads, marinades and sauces. And if you grow your own herbs, this is a great way to use them.

Good herbs for oils are thyme, marjoram, sage, fennel, basil and rosemary. Infused oils have the potential to support the growth of harmful bacteria, so follow the procedures listed carefully.

Suitable herbs for vinegars include dill, mint, thyme and rosemary. Vinegars made with berries give a sweet, delicate flavour; try nasturtiums and roses too.

Thyme & lemon oil

Ingredients
2 tablespoons fresh thyme leaves
Zest of 2 lemons
570ml (1 pint) light olive oil

Method
■ In a food processor, blend the thyme and lemon zest with half the olive oil until the mixture is well blended.

■ Pour into a wide-mouthed jar, top up with the remaining oil and secure the lid tightly.

■ Leave in a cool, dark place for three days. Shake once a day for the first two days to increase the flavour of the oil. On the third day, allow the herbs to settle. On the fourth day, strain the mixture through a funnel lined with a coffee filter.

■ Refrigerate the flavoured oil and use within three weeks.

Variation
Sage & orange oil
Use 3 tablespoons of fresh sage leaves and the zest of 2 oranges.

Rosemary, garlic & chilli oil

Ingredients

1 sprig (15cm/6in) fresh rosemary

4 cloves garlic

1–2 chilli peppers (according to taste)

½ teaspoon chilli powder

570ml (1 pint) light olive oil

Method

■ Bruise the rosemary sprig with the end of a wooden rolling pin.

■ Cut the garlic cloves in half.

■ Cut the chilli pepper in half lengthways.

■ Put the rosemary, garlic, chilli pepper and chilli powder into a clear 570ml (1 pint) glass bottle with a screw top.

■ Pour in the olive oil, secure the lid, shake well and refrigerate for two days before using. Keep the bottle stored in the fridge and use within one week.

Variation
Basil & garlic oil

Replace the rosemary with a handful of fresh basil, gently bruised in the same way. Omit the chilli pepper and powder.

Raspberry vinegar

Ingredients

110g (4oz) raspberries

570ml (1 pint) white wine vinegar

Method

■ Push the raspberries into a glass bottle, pour over the vinegar and fasten the lid.

■ Allow to stand in a cool, dark place for at least two weeks, shaking gently daily, before using.

■ Strain the berries out of the vinegar after two weeks if you wish, or leave them in.

Uses

Sprinkle the raspberry vinegar on fruit salads, or use as part of a salad dressing or with chicken.

Variation

Elderberry vinegar

Use three heads of elderberries: remove the berries from their cluster and lightly crush first.

Rose vinegar

Ingredients

4 dark, perfumed rose heads with the petals removed

570ml (1 pint) cider vinegar

Method

■ Place the petals in a glass jar with a tight-fitting lid.

■ Pour over the cider vinegar.

■ Fasten the lid securely and leave to macerate for two weeks in a cool, dark place.

■ Strain and bottle.

Uses

1 teaspoon of rose vinegar in 100ml (4 fl oz) water makes a refreshing, uplifting drink. Use also as a skin rinse for toning and energizing skin, or to lightly flavour fruit or cream dishes.

Nasturtium vinegar

Ingredients

6 nasturtium flowers

12 nasturtium seeds

6 nasturtium leaves

570ml (1 pint) cider vinegar

Method

■ Place all the ingredients in a glass jar and fasten with a tightly fitting lid.

■ Leave to macerate for one week in a cool, dark place.

■ Strain and bottle.

Uses

Nasturtiums add a sharp, peppery bite to vinegar. Use to dress winter salads of potato, red cabbage and celeriac.

SUPPORT LOCAL BUSINESSES

Air-freighting fresh produce has more than trebled in the past 20 years and, if the current shopping trends continue, we may soon arrive at a point where we'll have to rely on foreign imports for most of our everyday goods. Why not support local businesses by buying their seasonal free-range and organic produce, and help to reduce the environmental impact of imported food?

For those of us whose principle concern is our own or our children's health – but who are not and don't wish to be experts on nutrition – buying organic food is the easiest option. The organic standard, which requires a certification symbol or number on all organic produce, offers a genuine safety net, a basic protection against the worst of industrial food production ("farm fresh" usually means battery farmed).

For people who also care about fairness – fair and safe recompense for the producers of our daily foods – fair trade offers another basic standard. There are all kinds of reasons for this need for fair trading, the main one being that there are currently no laws to protect farmers. Large supermarkets can place whatever demands they want on farmers, who have to comply. And, at a time when concern about global warming has never been more widespread, these supermarkets are importing goods that, traditionally, were produced seasonally and more locally.

Simple ways to buy locally

By buying direct from the producers themselves wherever possible, you can recompense them fairly for their work. The best way to do this is to shop as locally as you can.

Box schemes Boxes of freshly grown seasonal vegetables and fruit that are sent directly to your home from the farmer or supplier. Most schemes in operation use locally grown produce from small farms, where the emphasis is on flavour and quality.

Local farmers' markets
Usually sited outdoors, these increasingly popular markets are one of the best ways to shop, as they offer masses of variety. They also give you a chance to meet the people who have produced what you are going to eat.

Small specialist shops
These independent shops provide a more pleasurable shopping experience than the fridge- and freezer-humming environments of supermarkets. The vendors invariably have a much better knowledge of the different products on sale.

Local food makes perfect sense

While fair standards, buying organic and reducing the amount of miles your food travels before it is consumed are all important reasons to shop ethically, if you believe in the value of choosing what you eat, and you care how it has been produced, then it's vital to support local farmers, shops and suppliers. In this way you can contribute to an increase in local market pressure on farmers to provide a greater diversity of locally produced food. There are, after all, only so many potatoes a local market can sell. And by diversifying their farms, farmers are necessarily moving to a more sustainable system of farming that will help to nourish the soil for generations to come.

The provenance of food

Most of the "nasties" – pesticides, fertilizers, antibiotics and hormones – used by commercial producers are designed to enable them to keep crops and animals in unnatural conditions. Diverse, free-range, small-scale farming techniques, on the other hand, automatically remove the need for these artificial props, and the worry that we might unknowingly be consuming harmful chemical residues. Free-range products bought locally can, therefore, be just as safe as organic produce that may have come from further away – with the advantage that you know where it has come from, and how it was grown or reared.

Facts on imported produce

● Air freighting is the fastest-growing form of food transport.

● Per kilometre, air freighting releases 50 times more CO_2 into the atmosphere than sea freighting, and ten times more CO_2 than lorries transporting goods by road.

● A kiwi fruit creates five times its own weight in CO_2 emissions when flown across the world.

● Although the UK could meet over 70% of its eating needs by using food produced in this country, currently half of all the food we consume is imported.

● In 2005, the UK exported just over £2.8 billion of goods to China, but imported nearly £16 billion of goods – a 30-fold increase on 1980.

CLEAN WITHOUT HARSH CHEMICALS

Most of us are in the habit of buying our cleaning products in the supermarket, so when we start to look for alternatives we usually turn back to the same supermarket shelves, where genuinely green alternatives are often pretty scarce. Why not break the habit and try making your own? The simplest ingredients from your kitchen are often all that is needed for the majority of household cleaning jobs.

Baking soda A versatile product that is safe enough to drink (it's a common heartburn remedy) and brush your teeth with (it has a gentle whitening action). Used dry, or mixed with water and a tiny squirt of washing-up liquid, it works as a disinfectant and mild abrasive that can remove hardened dirt and grease without scratching surfaces. It also softens water, so helping your other cleaners (including laundry detergents) clean and rinse off more effectively.

Vinegar Also known as acetic acid, vinegar is a mild acid that cuts though grease, disinfects and discourages mould. Useful for cleaning glass and tiles and removing the tea stains on cups. It is also an efficient air freshener.

Borax A useful mould and mildew remover and disinfectant, borax is also an effective water softener and can be used to whiten clothes. Use it sparingly on its own, mixed with a little water, or add some soap flakes. While it is a good cleaning product, use it with caution around children because, unlike baking soda, it is toxic if swallowed. Wear washing-up gloves when using borax.

Soap Real soap is made from natural products such as vegetable oils and animal fats. It is an effective cleaning agent that biodegrades quickly and has a minimal impact on the environment. Second best is an environmentally friendly washing-up liquid.

Microfibre cleaning cloths The basic purpose of detergents is to bring more water – one of the most efficient solvents in the world – into contact with whatever surface you are cleaning. Microfibres, which are finer than human hair and have amazing absorbency, effectively do the same thing. Used as directed they will leave most surfaces clean and dry. The most effective cloths have densely packed fibres.

DRY YOUR OWN HERBS

Harvest and dry your own herbs while they are full of the aromatic oils that give them their intense flavours, and have a supply for the kitchen for the rest of the year.

Some herbs, such as rosemary, thyme and bay, can be picked right through the winter, but most herbs either die down or are annuals and go to seed. The best way to preserve most leaves is by drying them (delicate leaves such as basil, chervil, dill and tarragon are better frozen). The best time is when the plant has formed its flower buds, but before the flowers have opened. This will vary from plant to plant so keep an eye on your herbs, and don't be shy about asking friends or relatives to snip off a few stalks from their plant if you spot a herb you don't have.

Harvest the leaves on a dry day, preferably in the morning before it gets too hot: strong sun causes leaf oils to evaporate.

Cut whole stalks using scissors or secateurs and dry as quickly as possible to keep the full flavour and colour. A warm (but not too hot) airy room is ideal for drying them.

Dry on a tray or wire rack, or on a piece of muslin stretched over and attached to a wooden frame, which you can make yourself. Take the leaves off the stalk, spread them out in a single layer and turn over occasionally as they are drying.

Once the leaves have become crispy and brittle, crumble them up, pour them into glass storage jars and label. Stored in a cool, dark cupboard, they should keep their flavour for about a year.

Drying tips

● If the herbs still have moisture in them when they are put into jars, they will go mouldy. Check the lids for the first few days and if you see moisture on the inside, tip out the herbs and dry off fully.

● Drying intensifies the flavour of herbs, making them three to four times more potent than fresh ones, so use them more sparingly in your cooking.

● Good for drying: sage, rosemary, bay, mint, lovage, thyme, marjoram, summer savory.

CHECK THE LABEL

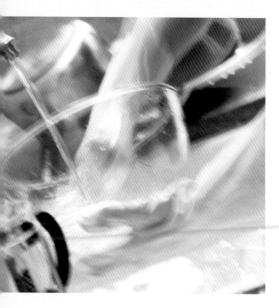

Indoor air pollution is a problem on the rise. Since most of us spend 90 per cent of our time indoors – in homes, offices and schools – pollutants can contribute substantially to poor health.

The air indoors can be compromised by any number of things, from the presence of a smoker to the use of formaldehyde-laden particleboard furnishings. But according to the US Environmental Protection Agency (EPA), a primary cause of indoor pollution is the use of conventional household cleaners.

Cleaning products

The problem is that in order to fulfil the increasingly ambitious claims for their products, manufacturers rely on combinations of chemicals that can be harsh and highly toxic. Many of these products easily evaporate or give off gases that can contaminate the air indoors. If a cleaner can instantly strip a kitchen tile of years of accumulated grease, what might it do to your skin or your body's cells if you happen to breathe it in, or to the natural environment?

Since household cleaners are not required to carry full ingredients labels, you will have to look for "signal words" that help to identify the kind of cleaner you are using. This table *(right)* identifies the names of some ingredients that may be listed in toxic products.

Check if it's toxic

You'll know a product is toxic if one of the following words, or something similar, is included on its label:

Hazardous

Corrosive

Inflammable

Warning

Caution

Danger

Irritant

Product	Look out for	Health effects
Air fresheners, furniture polishes	Parfum	Linked to asthma, nausea, mood changes, depression, skin irritation, lethargy, irritability, memory lapses.
All-purpose cleaners	Alcohol (incl. ethanol, methanol, isopropanol)	Nausea and vomiting if swallowed. Also found in washing-up liquid, glass and window cleaners.
	Propylene glycol	Irritant and immunotoxin. Also found in dishwashing detergents.
	Sodium tripolyphosphate	Skin, eye and lung irritant. Also found in laundry detergents.
Bathroom & toilet cleaners	Chlorine	Eye, skin and lung irritant. Major cause of poisonings in children. Also found in disinfectants, dishwasher tablets.
	Paradichlorobenzenes	Irritates eyes, nose, central nervous system. Also found in mildew control sprays, room deodorizers.
	Phenol	Extremely dangerous; suspected carcinogen; fatal if taken internally. Also found in disinfectants.
Degreasers	Butyl cellosolve	Liver, kidney, central nervous system damage. Also found in all-purpose cleaners, window cleaners.
Furniture polish	Formaldehyde	Highly toxic; known carcinogen. Also found in all-purpose cleaners, washing-up liquid, disinfectants, deodorizing sprays.
Glass & window cleaners	Ammonia	Fatal when swallowed. Also found in floor cleaners, furniture and metal polishes, disinfectants.
Limescale & rust removers	Hydrochloric acid	Corrosive, eye and skin irritant. Also found in toilet cleaners, metal polishes.
Metal & shoe polishes	Nitrobenzene	Causes skin discoloration, shallow breathing, vomiting, birth defects and death.
Oven & drain cleaners	Lye (sodium hydroxide)	Severe damage to stomach and oesophagus if swallowed. Also found in bathroom and toilet cleaners.
	Naphtha	Depresses the central nervous system.
Spot removers, dry-cleaning fluids	Trichloroethane	Damages liver and kidneys, narcotic. Also found in metal polishes, fabric cleaners, degreasers.

REDUCE, REUSE & RECYCLE

The average person in the West throws out their own body weight in rubbish every three months. Disposing of our domestic waste requires landfill space, increases the number of transportation lorries on our roads and creates pollution problems, so reducing the amount we throw away makes sense.

We are all being encouraged to recycle now, but recycling is only one way that we can minimize the rubbish we produce. Instead, think the "three Rs": reduce, reuse, and recycle.

Reduce your waste

Reducing the amount of rubbish we create is one of the best things we can do for the environment. Nearly all our waste comes from the things we buy, so reducing waste doesn't start at the bins, but at the shops. Almost 75 per cent of the rubbish generated in an average household is due to packaging.

- Choose products with the minimum amount of packaging.
- Buy your fruit and vegetables loose.
- Choose products with recyclable packaging.
- Buy larger pack sizes; one large pack uses less packaging than two small packets.
- Beware child-oriented packaging and "snack sizes". Make your own lunchbox portions and wrap them in greaseproof paper or reusable bags or containers.

Try the three Rs with shopping bags

Reduce
- Don't use new plastic carrier bags every time you shop. Instead, take a couple of strong jute or fabric bags with you – or use a backpack, which is the best way to carry the load and maintain your posture. Spread the weight between the two bags and hold a bag in each hand for balance.

Reuse
- Keep a few carrier bags in your handbag or in the car so that you can reuse them each time you go shopping.

- Reuse carrier bags in your bin instead of always buying new bin liners.

- Alternatively, take along any carrier bags you can't reuse to your local charity shop, which should be able to reuse them easily for you.

Recycle
- Only when your old carrier bags are worn out should you dispose of them. The best way to do this is at recycling collection points (which can now be found outside many supermarkets).

Reuse household items

Reusing items means giving them another lease of life before discarding
or recycling them.

■ Refill empty mineral water bottles with tap water. Wash the bottles regularly to prevent
a build-up of germs.

■ Take any unwanted clothes to charity shops, jumble sales, or clothing banks.

■ Children usually outgrow their clothes before they wear them out. Why not meet with
other parents to give away or swap your children's clothes?

■ Local communities are often in need of paint, wallpaper, and other excess household
items. Ask your local authority about what and how you can give unwanted items away.

■ Be inventive with your empty containers! Use plastic or tin containers to store kitchen
or household items, or to grow herbs, flowers or seeds.

Recycle to reduce energy consumption

The terms reusing and recycling are often confused, but recycling generally
means to re-form something. Recycled paper, for example, is first washed free
of ink, then pulped and squeezed out into new sheets. Certain plastics are
recycled into carpet fibres, garden furniture, agricultural pipes, dustbin bags,
clothes pegs, and so on. Metal and glass are recycled by melting the old material
in a furnace and remoulding it. Interestingly, recycling an aluminium can uses
only five per cent of the energy it would take to make a new can from mined
aluminium ore, and the energy saved is enough to power a TV for two hours. If
you don't have a recycling bin that is collected regularly by your local authority,
use your own separate bins or boxes to recycle glass, paper and plastic, if
possible, and take them to your local recycling depot or supermarket recycling
bin once they're full. Other household waste can also be recycled *(right)*.

So recycling as much as you can is better than using new – and reusing is
even better – but reducing our waste in the first place is the greenest option.
Remember, recycling industries only exist if there is a market for their
products. So buy recycled goods wherever you can.

What can you recycle?

■ **Paper and cardboard** Recycling paper doesn't just save trees, it saves significant amounts of water and electricity too.

■ **Glass** Glass can be recycled indefinitely.

■ **Plastic** Most plastic bottles are now made of PET, a recyclable plastic – look for the number 1 in a triangle on the base. Other recyclable plastic is coded with the letter (C) on the base.

■ **Textiles** Clothing banks may sell worn clothes as rags for engineering industries.

■ **Batteries** The toxic metals in batteries can contaminate groundwater. Take used batteries to appropriate collection points so that the metals can be retrieved.

■ **Metal** Aluminium from cans and foil is currently the most valuable of all recyclable waste.

■ **Compost** If you have an outdoor space, compost your kitchen and garden waste. Some local authorities collect waste for large-scale composting.

BAKE BREAD

If you bake your own organic bread, you have complete control over the ingredients you use. You can use different flours to make a variety of flavoured and textured breads, but wheat flour and a cultivated yeast will make the simplest of loaves. Try to source a local stoneground wheat flour, or use a granary flour.

Wheat contains the proteins glutenin and gliadin which, when combined with water and kneaded, produce gluten – elastic strands that trap the carbon dioxide made by the yeast and cause the bread to rise. It is impossible to give precise instructions for making bread, as different flours absorb variable amounts of liquid. The rising times will vary too, depending on the warmth of the room. In the following recipe you may need to add more water; the ideal dough is soft, but firm, in texture and you should be able to knead it easily.

Wholemeal bread (makes three loaves)

Ingredients

1.35kg (3lb) wholemeal flour
1 teaspoon salt
45g (1½oz) yeast
1 teaspoon honey
850ml (1½ pints) tepid water
3x450g (1lb) loaf tins

Method

■ Put the flour and salt into a bowl. Make a well in the centre.

■ Crumble in the yeast, add the honey and 100ml (4fl oz) of water, sprinkle flour over the well and leave in a warm place for 15 minutes.

■ Slowly mix in the rest of the water until you have a sticky, but quite firm, dough.

■ Turn out and knead gently for about 10 minutes until smooth. Pop the dough in a clean bowl, cover and leave in a warm place until it doubles in size (about 1½ hours).

■ Turn the dough out and divide into three. Shape the dough and place in oiled bread tins.

■ Cover with a cloth and leave for at least 40 minutes until the dough rises above the rim of the tin. Preheat the oven to 220°C/425°F/Gas 7.

■ Put the tins in the oven. After 40 minutes, remove. Tip out each loaf. Rap the base of a loaf with your knuckles; if it doesn't sound hollow, bake it for ten more minutes without the tin.

USE NATURAL NAPPIES

When disposable nappies were first sold, they seemed like a clever idea. Mums said goodbye to washing soiled cloth nappies and tossed the new plastic-lined disposables into the rubbish bin. We now know that more natural nappies are much better for your baby's skin, and for the environment.

Disposable nappies lined in plastic are made from synthetic fibres that contain deodorizing chemicals, bleaches and highly toxic dioxins, which are now known to be harmful to a baby's skin and to the environment. It is estimated that a plastic disposable nappy may take up to 500 years to biodegrade.

Kinder alternatives

Now the pendulum is swinging back to using cloth nappies and biodegradable disposables. Cloth nappies can be made from cotton, wool, silk, hemp and even bamboo fibres. Fitted cloth nappies that are easier to use are now available. They have velcro fastenings and disposable, flushable inner linings that make them just as waterproof and a great deal kinder to your baby's skin. They are also more absorbent than plastic nappies.

There are also new types of disposables available, which are made from more natural, chlorine-free, biodegradeable constituents that don't make use of super absorbent gels *(right)*, and are free from perfumes and other harmful chemicals.

The average baby will get through approximately 5,000 nappies. Advantages of using nappies made from natural fibres include:

No chemicals Cloth and biodegradable nappies contain no harmful bleaches, dyes and hormone-disrupting chemicals. Plastic-lined disposables contain a super-absorbent gelling material known as sodium polyacrylate, which can soak up 30 times its own weight in liquid. This gel releases an oestrogen-like chemical close to the baby's skin.

Less nappy rash The absorbent gel material in plastic disposables can make a nappy feel dry even when it is wet. As a result, parents may be tempted to leave their baby in a nappy for longer. This exposes your baby to ammonia, which urine produces as it breaks down, and which can irritate skin and produce nappy rash.

Economy Washed carefully, as you would any other item of clothing, cotton nappies should last you through two (or more) children. Cloth nappies can be washed and reused up to 200 times, and then used as lint-free cleaning rags.

Preserving the earth's resources The manufacturing process involved in producing biodegradable disposable nappies does far less harm to the environment than plastic disposables because no bleaching agents are used.

The facts on plastic disposables

● Every day in the UK alone, 9 million disposable nappies are tipped into landfill sites. It is estimated that nappy waste comprises 4% of all household waste.

● Viruses in soiled disposable nappes can survive for over two weeks, and run-off from landfills containing disposable nappies can contaminate groundwater supplies.

● Plastic disposables use 3½ times more total energy, 8 times more non-renewable materials and 90 times more renewable materials than cloth nappies. They produce 60 times more solid waste and use 25% more land for growing the materials used in their manufacture.

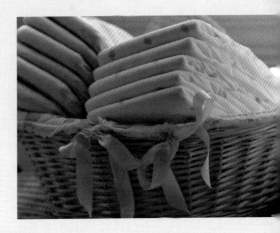

FORAGE FOR WILD GREENS

If you don't have room for more than a couple of herbs or leafy vegetables in your window boxes, you can still enjoy herby soups, dishes of spinach-like greens and salads with a selection of tangy leaves by collecting wild greens.

The leaves that you can gather in the wild won't have been "improved" or artificially fertilized; they will provide you with an array of different tastes and textures; and, of course, they're free. It may take you half a day of foraging to pick enough leaves for a soup or dish, but it's a wonderful way of getting to know the wild plants of an area and discover the tastes our ancestors enjoyed long before we bought our vegetables at supermarkets. You can find edible greens almost all year round (in a mild winter you should be able to pick enough chickweed shoots, hairy bittercress and Jack-by-the-hedge to transform a lettuce-only salad) and in all sort of places, from marshy spots to woods, grassy areas, hedgerows and even waste ground. Just make sure that you never strip an area bare or uproot plants.

Many wild plants are edible, but they have a much more bitter flavour than we're used to so try small amounts to start with. For example, the sharpness of dandelion leaves, picked before the flowers come out, is definitely an acquired taste. On the other hand, sweet cicely has sugary leaves that combine deliciously with stewed fruit.

Safe picking and eating

● Only pick a plant if you're 100% sure of what it is. Whether you're new to foraging or not, always take a couple of reliable botanical field guides with you.

● Don't pick from any areas that might have been sprayed with weedkiller or insecticide, or from the verges of heavily used roads.

● Don't pick discoloured or withered leaves.

● If you have never eaten a particular plant before, try just a small amount the first time you eat it in case it disagrees with you.

Twelve of the best wild greens

① Chickweed *(Stellaria media)*
A tender wild green, with a taste like corn salad, that can be picked all year except when frosty. Add to salads.

② Common nettle *(Urtica dioica)*
Rich in vitamins A and C, the leaves are best picked young and cooked like spinach or made into a soup.

③ Jack-by-the-hedge *(Alliara petiolata)*
Pick a few young leaves from each plant. Finely chop them and add to salads for a mildly garlic flavour.

④ Wild thyme *(Thymus drucei)*
Pick when in flower and use raw to make a tisane, or in soups and cooked dishes. Milder than the cultivated varieties.

⑤ Hairy bittercress *(Cardamine hirsuta)*
The leaves of this plant have a sweet, tangy flavour and can be used in salads and sandwiches.

⑥ Alexanders *(Smyrnium olusatrum)*
The spicy young leaves can be added to salads, and the pinkish part of the stems can be boiled and eaten like asparagus.

7 Common sorrel (*Rumex acetosa)*
The sharp-tasting leaves can be added to salads and cooked dishes.

8 Watercress
(*Rorippa nasturtium-aquaticum)*
This tastes just like the plants that are grown commercially. For a stronger flavour, pick the older, darker leaves, but make sure the plant grows in clean, fast flowing water.

9 Good King Henry
(*Chenopodium bonus-henricus*)
This is a perennial, which can be picked almost all year round and cooked like spinach or added to soups.

10 Hop *(Humulus lupulus)*
Pick the young shoots and leaves in late spring and early summer. Add to soups and omelettes, or soak in salt water for an hour and blanch until tender.

11 Fat hen (*Chenopodium album)*
This plant rapidly colonizes waste ground. The leaves are best cooked like spinach.

12 Fennel (*Foeniculum vulgare)*
Cut the leaves early in the summer and add to fish dishes and potato salads.

NOURISH SKIN NATURALLY

The simpler your skincare regime, the better. Conventional skin creams and lotions can contain mixtures of 20 or more synthetic ingredients, many of which are of no direct benefit to your skin. Instead, they are necessary to hold mixtures of incompatible ingredients, such as oil and water, together and to extend the product's shelf life.

When you buy a conventional skin care product you are buying a quick fix, something that may well produce a fast, temporary result – for instance, visible results in an hour – but which doesn't actually do anything to improve your skin in the long term.

Organic products tend to be much more straightforward mixtures that work in a different way. The organic plant-based ingredients tend to have higher levels of naturally occurring vitamins and trace elements of essential fatty acids – all the things that your skin needs to nourish and protect it.

As an alternative to mineral oil-based products, which are derived from petroleum, why not consider using simple, natural plant- or animal-based oils to maintain your skin's natural moisture balance? Many of these oils, such as jojoba and emu, are amazingly similar to the oils in human skin and as such are non-irritating, won't clog pores and are deeply nourishing. Better still, they do the same job at a fraction of the price of commercial brands, and you'll have the advantage of knowing what you are using on your skin.

Choose organic products

If you still prefer to buy your skincare products, make sure that they are organic. Encourage your local shops to sell safer products and read and learn to understand the label. Avoid any skin products that contain these ingredients:

- Butylparaben (and other parabens)
- Parafinnum liquidum
- Cyclomethicone
- Parfum

Beneficial oils for your skin

Apply a small amount of your chosen oil with damp hands, or after bathing, to keep your skin soft and protected.

For younger skin

Apricot kernel oil

Coconut oil

Hemp seed oil

Wheat germ oil

Olive oil

For more mature skin

Avocado oil

Evening primrose oil

Rosa mosqueta oil

For any skin type

Almond oil

Cocoa butter

Emu oil

Jojoba

Squalene

Home-made scrub

Make a simple exfoliating scrub for your body or face by mixing a natural oil (olive oil is a good choice) with honey and sugar. If you have sensitive skin, use ground oatmeal instead of sugar for a gentler exfoliating action. Don't use exfoliating products too often: once a week is enough.

USE SAFER PEST CONTROLS AT HOME

Sharing our homes with rodents, insects or other uninvited creatures can be unpleasant, and occasionally dangerous. But before you reach for the nearest commercial pesticide, try some safer alternatives.

Householders in the UK use over 4,000 tonnes of commercial pesticides each year. Often, though, the potential harm pests cause in the home is outweighed by the toxicity of the chemicals in these pesticide products: powders, for example, can irritate the lungs, even if the product is not labelled as toxic (it's important to note that you should always read the label of any pest control product). And not all creatures that come into our homes and gardens are pests. Some, such as spiders, can be beneficial as they eat flies and mosquitoes, while wasps kill many garden pests.

Basic principles

The first rule of pest management is to avoid encouraging any pests in the first place. Seal all cracks and holes in walls, floors or skirting where mice or insects could enter (rodents won't chew through wire wool), and consider fitting fly-screens over doors, windows and vents.

Simple preventative measures

■ Keep food in tightly sealed jars or plastic boxes, not open packets.

■ Keep floors and surfaces clean – wipe up crumbs and sticky spills quickly.

■ Rinse food and drink containers before throwing them away or recycling them.

■ Keep your rubbish bins covered and empty them regularly.

If these four simple preventative measures don't work, try the following non-toxic or "least toxic" methods of killing or discouraging pests.

Ants

■ Stop ants reaching pet food by placing the food bowl in a shallow container filled with soapy water, making a moat that the ants cannot cross.

■ Try crushing and sprinkling pennyroyal, sage, mint, thyme or bay leaves, paprika or cinnamon across ant paths.

■ Boric acid and borate-based products available at garden centres are effective (a natural product, boric acid is far less toxic than chemical pesticides, but it is mildly harmful if ingested so use it sparingly).

Clothes moths

■ Washing clothes at high temperature kills the eggs and larvae, or put woollen clothes in a freezer for 72 hours.

■ Store clothes made from natural fibres in airtight bags.

■ Place sachets of lavender or cedarwood chips amongst stored clothes.

■ Pheromone traps will catch adult moths, but not the damage-causing grubs.

Mosquitoes

■ Protect yourself and your rooms: use a spray bottle filled with ten drops of essential oil (try cedarwood, lemongrass, peppermint, citronella or eucalyptus) and 115ml (4fl oz) of water.

■ Mosquitoes don't like breezes, so use a fan.

■ Sleep under a mosquito net.

■ Limit mosquito breeding places by keeping lids on water butts, emptying standing water from old flower pots, etc.

Herbal flea collar

1 untreated soft felt collar

Mix together:

2 teaspoons pure alcohol
1 tablespoon rosemary
essential oil
1 tablespoon lemon verbena
essential oil
1 tablespoon lavender
essential oil
1 tablespoon pennyroyal
essential oil
Oil of 4 garlic capsules

Soak the flea collar thoroughly in the mixture, then dry. The effect lasts for one month.

Rats & mice

■ There are many types of trap available. Some are lethal, others are humane, allowing you to release mice outdoors.

■ Pet cats keep mice down, terrier dogs may keep rats at bay.

Fleas

■ Use a flea comb on your pet. Drown any fleas you catch in soapy water.

■ Clean bedding and vacuum your home regularly.

■ Use essential oils to make a flea collar *(left)*.

Food moths

■ Some food moth grubs eat flour, cereals and many other foods. Seal and throw away any contaminated food.

■ Grubs can even chew through packaging, so inspect unopened boxes.

■ The grubs can crawl up walls and into cracks before they pupate. Use a vacuum cleaner to get right into these spots.

■ The "outdoor" moths that fly into the house at night will not cause problems.

Cockroaches

■ Dust boric acid into the cracks where cockroaches shelter.

■ Diatomaceous earth is a dust that scratches the waterproof coat of cockroaches and other crawling insects, causing them to dry out and die.

House flies

■ Use fly screens made of chain links or beads in doorways.

■ Old-fashioned muslin covers prevent flies settling on food.

■ Try hanging a sweet basil plant by a window or back door.

Homemade fly paper

Mix together equal parts by volume of sugar, golden syrup and water. Boil the mixture until thick, stirring occasionally.

Leave to cool, then dip strips of brown parcel wrapping tape into the sticky mixture. Leave to dry outside for about 30 minutes.

Hang up with string. The flies will be attracted to, and trapped on, the sticky coating.

■ Fly-paper or sticky strips are effective. Home-made versions *(above)* won't give off toxic fumes or bad odours.

■ UV lights and electronic "zappers" work, but do use up energy.

Wasps

■ Don't leave sweet food or drinks out.

■ Buy a wasp trap, or make your own using a bottle or jar. Wasps like sweet food, so mix jam with water and a drop of detergent to bait your trap. The detergent helps to kill them.

■ Wasps in wasps' nests die over winter so leave them alone if they are not bothering you.

GROW STRAWBERRIES IN A HANGING BASKET

Fill a hanging basket with strawberry plants, hang it somewhere sheltered and sunny and enjoy pretty white flowers in early summer followed by lots of juicy red fruits. A hanging basket is an ideal way of growing strawberries, as it keeps the fruit off the ground and so is much less likely to suffer from pests (such as slugs) and diseases.

It's a good idea to line the basket with porous material – you could use a piece of sacking or hessian – and then make an inner lining from some plastic with holes punched in it.
■ Make up a mixture of multipurpose compost and loam (in about equal amounts), with a couple of handfuls of grit and some bonemeal forked into it, and fill the basket. For a large basket buy five or six plants in spring, plant them and water well.

Once the plants start to grow, feed them with a liquid fertiliser that's high in potassium, such as tomato food, every 10–14 days. Keep well watered, and daily in hot weather.

Once you've picked all the fruit, the plants will stop growing for a few weeks. Then in early autumn they will make more crowns again in preparation for the next year. You should be able to keep your plants going for three seasons before replacing them. Don't forget to refresh the compost every spring.

If you have space for another basket, you could propagate another batch of strawberry plants and get more berries for the following year. Strawberries make new plantlets at the end of runners. Hang the second basket right next to the first one. In early autumn lift up several of the runners from the main basket and lay the plantlets onto the compost of the second one. Pin down each runner with some galvanised wire.

After a few weeks when the new plants have rooted (gently tug to check), cut the runners that attach them to the mother plant.

Or grow tomatoes

If you are not a fan of strawberries, try growing cherry tomatoes instead. Varieties such as the red "Tumbler" or the yellow "Tumbling Tom Yellow" are ideal for hanging baskets.

● Use one plant in a small basket (25cm/10in diameter), three in a large basket.

● Use loam-based compost. Add some water-storing gel or granules and grit for drainage.

● Feed with tomato fertilizer little and often.

● Water frequently, especially during hot weather. Don't leave standing in water, as waterlogging causes the fruit to split.

● Pick when ripe. At the end of the season pick off the last tomatoes and ripen indoors.

TRAVEL WISELY

Moving products and people from place to place is an essential part of modern life, but many forms of transport, plus the sheer scale of our transport infrastructure, are causing problems to our health and environment.

Road traffic and air travel are the fastest-growing sources of the main greenhouse gas, carbon dioxide. Exhaust pollution can aggravate lung and breathing problems, and traffic accidents are all too common. Road traffic and aircraft noise can disrupt daily life, and roads and runways now cover great tracts of countryside. By changing some of our transport decisions, however, we can not only reduce our impact on the planet but improve our health too.

Rather than drive everywhere in your car, try other options such as walking or cycling: a brisk 20 minute walk will give you a good aerobic work-out, while people who cycle regularly typically have a fitness level equivalent to someone who is ten years younger.

Reduce your car usage

■ If everyone replaced just one return car journey per week with another form of travel, traffic on the roads would be reduced by more than ten per cent.

■ If one of your regular journeys is the school run, how about organizing a "walking bus" scheme, where two or more adults collect children and escort them along a pre-arranged pedestrian route to school?

■ If you drive to work, could you arrange a car-share scheme? Many companies now offer preferential parking or other incentives to discourage individual car commuting.

■ Plan to get as much as you can out of a car journey. One trip to undertake five tasks is better for the environment than five separate car trips.

Facts on travel

● Half of all car journeys made are less than 2.5km (2 miles).

● 60% of all car journeys have only one person in the car.

● Nearly 70% of all flights within Europen airspace are less than 1,000km (620 miles).

● An aeroplane creates three times more CO_2 and pollution than a train on distances less than 500km (300 miles).

● Globally, aircraft generate more than 700 million tonnes of CO_2 per year.

● A passenger taking a long-haul return flight from the UK to the US produces as much CO_2 as a motorist does driving in the UK for a year.

Tips for greener driving

Limit the use of air conditioning in your car, as it uses up more fuel.

Reduce the weight of your car by unloading any heavy items you won't need on the journey.

Drive with the windows up, and remove the roof-rack if you aren't using it. This reduces drag and makes your fuel consumption more efficient.

Check that your tyres are inflated to the correct tyre pressure. For every 6psi the tyre is under-inflated, the fuel consumption increases by one per cent.

Consider converting your car so that it can use LPG (Liquid Petroleum Gas) or biofuels. These fuels are much less polluting than petrol, and are becoming increasingly available.

Keep your speed down It can cost you up to 25 per cent more in fuel to drive at 110 kmph (70mph) compared to 80kmph (50mph).

Harsh acceleration and braking can use up to 30 per cent more fuel.

Avoid unnecessary revving or idling of the engine. It's more efficient to turn your engine off if you are stuck in a traffic jam.

A well-tuned engine improves a car's performance and limits fuel consumption.

Consider buying a small, efficient car for your everyday needs, and taking the train or renting a larger car for longer journeys when you need it. Driving a 12mpg (miles per gallon) 4x4 car rather than a 25mpg car can waste more energy in one year than leaving the fridge door open for seven years.

Consider using a hybrid vehicle, which saves energy by using an electric battery as well as petrol.

Thinking about a holiday?

Artificially cheap flights may make you feel that holidays on sunny coasts or weekend city breaks abroad are almost obligatory. But there are other options. You could:

- Take a train.
- Go by boat. A cruise is possibly the most relaxing start to any holiday.
- Explore your own country and discover new areas.

Air travel

Aircraft release more than 600 million tonnes of the world's major greenhouse gas, carbon dioxide, into the atmosphere each year. They also release other greenhouse gases, including nitrogen oxides (NOx) and water vapour. These have a more significant effect on the climate when emitted at altitude than at ground level. Aircraft vapour trails, or contrails, can also encourage the formation of cirrus clouds. Both contrails and cirrus clouds warm the earth's surface, magnifying the global warming effect of aviation.

Although aircraft and engine technology is improving, this will not offset the projected growth in aircraft emissions. The only way to reduce aircraft greenhouse gas emissions is to fly less.

Hidden transport costs

It isn't just the journeys that you personally make that have an impact on the planet. The products you buy also have hidden transport costs. Flying 1kg (2lb 4oz) of asparagus from California to the UK uses 900 times more energy than the home-grown equivalent, and food transport is responsible for around a quarter of the lorries on our roads.

Buy locally produced food wherever you can to help to reduce "food miles" – the total distance that food is transported from field to plate.

How efficient is your journey?

In terms of the amount of fossil fuels burnt, cars and planes are very inefficient ways to travel. Buses and trains are much less polluting.

g carbon dioxide per passenger kilometre	
Train	73
Bus	77
Car	114
Plane	330
(short-haul flights)	

MAKE & FREEZE BABY FOODS

How and what we eat as babies and toddlers can have a huge influence on our long-term health. Poor nutrition in childhood has been shown to cause heart disease and diabetes in adults. Make the most of local seasonal fruit and vegetables and turn them into simple, nutritious meals for your child.

Frozen baby food has a better flavour than organic jars, and is preservative-free. Use small, sealable containers to fill the freezer with individual portions. Defrost them thoroughly before reheating and feeding them to your child. Always make smoothies fresh.

Courgette & tomato scones

(from 12 months old)
If you freeze the scones, use within one month.

Ingredients

350g (12oz) self-raising wholemeal flour
1 teaspoon baking powder
50g (2oz) butter
50g (2oz) courgette, grated
2 sundried tomatoes, finely chopped
1 teaspoon fresh thyme, chopped
275ml (½ pint) milk

Method

■ Put the flour and baking powder in a bowl. Rub in the butter.

■ Stir in the courgette, tomatoes, thyme and enough milk to make a manageable dough.

■ Roll out the dough until it is about 2cm (¾in) thick. Cut into rounds. Place on an oiled baking tray and bake for 12–15 minutes at 180°C/350°F/Gas 4.

Variation
Red pepper & olive scones

Use 1 finely diced red pepper and 8 black olives, pitted and finely chopped.

Herb mash

(from 8 months old)

Use a mix of whatever fresh herbs you have to hand – parsley, chives, fennel and tarragon are all good choices. The garlic and beetroot mashes freeze well, but the herb mash doesn't.

Ingredients

2 large potatoes, washed and pricked
2 tablespoons fresh herbs, chopped
A knob of butter and a splash of olive oil

Method

■ Bake the potatoes in an oven at 220°C/425°F/Gas 7 for about 1½ hours.

■ When cooked, split in half, scoop the potato into a bowl and mash. Stir in the herbs, butter and oil. If the mix is dry, add a little rice milk.

Variations

Garlic mash Omit the herbs. Soften 2 finely chopped cloves of garlic in the olive oil and butter before stirring into the mashed potato.

Beetroot mash Bake a beetroot at the same as the potatoes. Skin the beetroot and mash it with the potato, or process to a purée first. The mixture should be soft enough without adding rice milk.

Carrot soup with ginger

(from 8 months old)

Both the carrot soup and the parsnip variation will freeze well. Use small containers with well-fitting lids and eat within one month of freezing. Served with a chunk of fresh bread, these soups make a satisfying supper for older children and adults too.

Ingredients

50g (2oz) butter

700g (1½lb) carrots, washed and chopped

1 medium onion, chopped

2.5cm (1in) cube fresh root ginger, grated

1.2 litres (2 pints) salt-free vegetable stock

Method

■ Melt the butter in a thick-bottomed pan, then stir in the chopped carrots and onion. Sweat gently for five minutes.

■ Stir in the grated ginger and cook for a further three minutes.

■ Add the stock and simmer, with the pan covered, for 15 minutes.

■ Cool slightly, then process the mixture in a blender until smooth.

Serve with a swirl of fresh yoghurt or a scattering of freshly chopped parsley.

Variation

Parsnip soup with ginger Replace the carrots with 700g (1½lb) parsnips and cook according to the same method.

Barley & vegetable casserole

(from 10 months old)

This dish is delicious fresh or frozen.

Ingredients

2 tablespoons olive oil

2 cloves garlic, peeled and chopped

1 onion, diced

1 small parsnip, diced

1 medium carrot, diced

1 small celeriac, diced

50g (2oz) pot barley

570fl oz (1 pint) salt-free vegetable stock

Method

■ Heat the oil in a thick-bottomed pan. Cook the garlic gently in the oil for a few minutes.

■ Add the vegetables and stir for two minutes, then add the barley and stock.

■ Bring to the boil, reduce the heat and simmer gently for 40 minutes.

■ Mash lightly if required and serve.

Variation

Chickpea & vegetable casserole Replace the pot barley with chickpeas which, if dried, need soaking for 24 hours before using.

Banana & raspberry smoothie

(from 8 months old)

None of these drinks are suitable for freezing.

Ingredients

1 banana, peeled, sliced and frozen

1 large handful (150g/5oz) fresh raspberries

150ml (5fl oz) apple juice

Method

■ Put all the ingredients in a blender.

■ Cover and process on a low speed until smooth.

■ Pour the smoothie into a suitable container for your baby, decant the rest into a glass for yourself, and serve.

Variations

Banana & strawberry smoothie

Replace raspberries with strawberries.

Banana & blackberry smoothie

Replace raspberries with blackberries.

Fruit & protein smoothie For babies over 18 months, replace the apple juice with almond milk made by processing blanched almonds and water (in a ratio of 1:3) in a blender until very smooth.

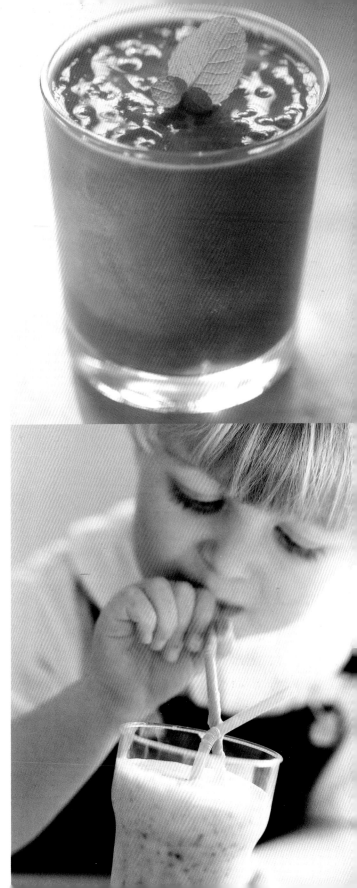

CHOOSE NATURAL FACE & BODY PRODUCTS

It's important to use toiletries and cosmetics that are as pure as possible. There are literally hundreds of chemicals that go into conventional face and body products and while not all the ingredients are bad for you, some are.

The best way to avoid unhealthy chemicals in your products is to read and to learn to understand what is on the label. The most harmful ingredients tend to be those that are added to make a product last longer – for example, preservatives; or to make it feel nicer on the skin, such as mineral oils and silicones; or give it a "signature" scent, like perfumes. These ingredients impart no actual benefit to your skin and can be quite

Product	Ingredient	What to look for	Worrying effects
Antibacterial facewash	Bacteriocides	Triclosan, Benzalkonium chloride, Chlorohexidine	Skin irritation, promotes bacterial resistance. Also found in toothpaste and mouthwash.
Deodorants	Aluminium	Aluminium chlorohydrate, Aluminium zirconium	Neurotoxin linked to Alzheimer's disease. May also contribute to heart and lung disease and fertility problems. Also found in make-up products.
Face & body lotions	Mineral oils	Parafinnum liquidum, Petrolatum	Skin irritants, allergens, potential carcinogens. Also found in baby oils and lipsticks.
	Silicones	Cyclomethicone, Dimethicone, Simethicone, Cyclopentasiloxane, Dimethicone	Skin irritation, blocked pores. Some silicones are tumour promoters and accumulate in liver and lymph nodes. Non-biodegradable. Also found in hair conditioners and most make-up.
	Preservatives	Parabens (methylparaben, ethylparaben, butylparaben, propylparaben, etc.), EDTA, Formaldehyde, Quaternium 15, Methylisothiazolinone	Skin irritation and allergic reactions. Can be neurotoxic. Some, like parabens, are suspected hormone disrupters. Also found in all cosmetics and toiletries.

toxic. Some, like harsh detergents and antibacterial agents, are just plain unnecessary – you can get the job done with much milder ingredients and better attention to hygiene.

When you buy toiletries and cosmetics, buy organic products that are free from synthetic preservatives, fragrances, colours, and so on. Use this table to help you identify those ingredients it would be wise to avoid.

Product	Ingredient	What to look for	Worrying effects
Hairspray	Phthalates	Dibutyl phthalate (DBP), Diethylhexyl phthalate (DEHP)	Hormone-disrupting plasticisers that "fix" the fragrance onto the skin. Can cause damage to liver, lungs and kidneys. May affect fertility and foetal development. Also found in nail varnish and perfumed products.
Perfumed products	Fragrances	Parfum	Parfum is a mixture of dozens of synthetic chemicals that are linked to asthma, skin irritation, nausea, mood changes, depression, lethargy, irritability and memory lapses.
Shampoo & bodywash	Detergents	Sodium lauryl sulphate, Cocamidopropyl betaine, Ammonium lauryl sulphate, Cocamide DEA, Cocamide MEA	Skin irritation. Can promote the formation of cancer-causing substances known as nitrosamines in products during storage. Also found in bubble bath and liquid hand soaps.
Suncare products	Sunscreens	Benzophenone-3, Homosalate, 4-methyl-benzylidene camphor (4-MBC), Octyl-methoxycinnamate, Octyl-dimethyl-PABA, Octocrylene	Hormone-disrupting chemicals known to affect the fertility of animals in the wild. Also found in moisturisers, lipsticks and foundations.

CAMPAIGN!

We can all do things in our everyday lives that help to change the world for the better. But the biggest changes happen when other people come on board too – particularly those who make policy decisions.

Campaigning tools

Choose a method that suits your cause and your audience.

Letters and emails to decision-makers, opinion formers or local newspapers explain and argue the case for your cause.

Petitions raise and demonstrate support.

Leaflets help to present information about your campaign in a simple and accessible way.

Demonstrations can be a great way to get publicity, as long as they are perceived positively.

Direct action, such as boycotting goods, has a direct impact on the situation, as well as getting publicity.

The media – newspapers, radio and television – can be used to reach a large audience and publicise an event, raise support, or share news of your successes.

A good campaign needs planning. You should think carefully about what you want to achieve, how you are going to do it and how long it should take.

Work out your goals

You need to work out exactly what you are trying to achieve – and be able to explain it simply – so that:
- Other people can sign up to your campaign
- You focus your energies
- You can work out what you need to do
- You know when you've done it!

Make a strong case

To have an impact on the people you want to influence, you must demonstrate why your issue matters to them. You will need to gather evidence and get as much accurate information as possible to support your case.

How to achieve your aims

Working together The greatest resource of a campaign is the number of people prepared to take part.
- You will probably need to build a team of people to help.
- You should also build partnerships with other groups, local societies, local businesses, supporters, and so on.
- Ensure that everyone involved is giving the same message.

Learn how decisions are made Find out who makes the decisions, and who influences them. Local politicians will study local newspapers. Businesses listen to their customers.

Find out when decisions are made For instance, when are your local elections or key company meetings?

Feeling overwhelmed?

Some problems may seem too huge for you to make any impact, but every problem has a local angle. If you are concerned about climate change, for example, you could start by looking at how much carbon dioxide your household, company or town produces – then challenge people to do something about it.

Get your message across

Depending on your issue, you might need to reach decision makers, influencers and supporters.

They could include:

- Your local authority
- Central government
- Trade unions
- Local businesses
- Global corporations
- Campaign groups
- The media
- Your local community
- Local schools
- Local celebrities

How to write a campaign letter

- Try to find the name of a relevant, influential person.
- Introduce yourself.
- Make your message brief and give a positive solution.
- Include some brief facts and background information.
- Always ask for an answer.
- Keep it short. If more information is needed, add background notes, such as references to relevant magazine articles, and so on.
- File it. Keep copies of letters and responses.

MAKE FRUIT & FLOWER CORDIALS

Why not make cordials with berries and flowers so that you can enjoy the deliciously light taste of summer long after the season is over? Made and stored properly, these concentrated syrups should last several months, and will make great presents.

There is nothing quite as refreshing as the delicately scented taste of an elderflower cordial, particularly if it is home-made using hand-picked elderflowers. Clusters of the small white or cream flowers appear in late spring; use freshly-picked flowers for the best taste. Or gather fresh berries and make all sorts of alternative flavours.

Cordials make delicious pure fruit drinks when added to still or sparkling water or lemonade, or try mixing elderflower cordial with white wine and sparkling water for a sensationally different spritzer. The concentrated syrups can also be used to enhance desserts or make sorbets and mousses.

Basic cordial recipe

(makes 1 litre/1¾ pints)

Ingredients

15 large heads of elderflower, or 500g (1lb 1oz) fresh fruit, such as strawberries, raspberries, blackberries or blueberries

500ml (17fl oz) water

1 lemon

900g (2lb) caster sugar

40g (1½oz) tartaric/citric acid

Method

■ If using berries, crush them slightly first, as this helps to release the flavours.

■ In a clean pan bring the water to the boil.

■ Meanwhile, slice the lemon thinly and place in a large glass bowl along with the elderflower heads or berries, sugar and tartaric/citric acid.

■ As soon as the water has boiled, pour it into the bowl and stir until all the sugar has dissolved.

■ Leave the bowl to cool, then cover and place somewhere cool and dark for four days.

■ Using a clean spoon, taste the concentrate to see if it is strong enough. If it requires further steeping, leave it in the fridge for another day or so.

■ Strain through a sieve lined with muslin.

■ Decant into sterilized bottles. Keeps in the fridge for up to six months.

USE NATURAL CLEANERS & POLISHES

As we scrub and polish to keep dirt and germs at bay, many of the products we use are actually more risky than the germs and dirt themselves. Use environmentally-friendly cleaners instead.

It is ironic that while most modern cleaning products remove surface dirt and sometimes germs, they also make the air and surfaces dirty with industrial chemicals, hydrocarbons, chlorine and more. But what could green cleaning possibly have to offer that would compete with today's modern formulations?

■ **A cleaner home** Instead of washing away dirt with synthetic chemicals, or masking unpleasant smells with heavy perfumes (which can trigger asthma and headaches), you'll be getting your home really clean.

■ **It costs less** Using readily available ingredients, such as vinegar, means that you will spend less money on cleaners.

■ **Nothing dangerous under the sink** A much safer way to live, especially if you have children. You can clean most floors with hot water and a tiny amount of eco-friendly washing-up liquid, giving them a good rinse afterwards, or try making your own floor cleaner *(right)*.

Wooden floor polishes

Wood flooring is the epitome of unadulterated naturalness. Compared to carpeting, wood is a cleaner flooring that helps keep levels of allergenic dust mites down and requires fewer cleaners to keep it looking good. It doesn't need "nourishing" or "feeding";

Floor cleaner recipe

In a bucket of water mix together:

¼ cup liquid soap

½–1 cup distilled vinegar or lemon juice

To enhance the fragrance, you can add 1 cup of strong, freshly brewed herb tea of your choice.

instead, an occasional polish keeps the wood looking nice and prevents it from losing moisture. However, most commercial wood floor polishes contain flammable and neurotoxic ingredients. The health problems most often associated with polishes – everything from headaches to depression and asthma – are due to the inhalation of fumes or vapours.

Unvarnished wood can be cleaned and polished easily and beautifully with very simple compounds. A dab of vinegar on a slightly damp cloth is an effective cleaner, while a little light olive oil on a cloth will polish and protect your wood. Or make your own beeswax polish *(below)*. Apply it sparingly with a lint-free cloth (microfibre cloths are ideal) and buff well.

Make your own wooden floor polish

Grate ¼ cup beeswax into a small ceramic bowl or glass-measuring cup (grating helps to speed up the melting process). Put the bowl into a shallow pan of boiling water.

When the beeswax has completely melted, remove it from the heat and slowly add ¼ cup of turpentine. Mix thoroughly. Turpentine, made from the resin of coniferous trees, is an environmentally-friendly solvent.

Transfer the mixture to a small, clean screw-top jar or pot. Terpentine can have a strong odour so add a few drops of lavender, orange, lemon, pine oil or other aromatic essential oil extract to the mix when the polish is cool, but still soft.

GIVE ECO PRESENTS

When it comes to buying presents, we may not always be as ecologically minded as we are with other purchases, but an original, thoughtfully chosen present that makes a positive difference to the environment can be just as pleasurable to give.

1 **Tree – a gift for life** Dedicate a tree in someone's honour, or give a "Grow-a-tree" kit.

2 **Solar-powered gadget** Use the sun's free, renewable and endless supply of energy to power an iPod or charge a mobile phone. Good for people who are always on the go.

3 **Home-made jams & pies** Choose your favourite recipe and get to work in the kitchen. The best part is designing your own labels.

4 **Water butt** Collects and stores rainwater for watering the garden. Reduces mains water consumption, as well as water bills.

5 **Vegetable & fruit box scheme** Kick-start a food revolution by giving a trial month's worth of local, organic food grown by small producers. It's healthy, delicious and good for the environment.

6 **Organic linens** Soft, cosy and luxurious, organic bed sheets, duvets and pillowcases are made from organic raw materials produced without harsh chemical treatments.

7 **Bicycle** Harness a loved one's pedal power with a new, upgraded, or second-hand bike.

8 **Wooden toys for children** Plastics are used in 80 per cent of new toys; eschew plastic and PVC toys and choose natural wood next time you shop for children's toys.

9 **"No sweat" trainers** Fashionable trainers made by fair-trade labour and using rubber soles from sustainably managed forests

10 **Foraged produce** It takes time and effort to forage for edibles, which will surely be appreciated by the recipient of a jar full of chestnuts or a punnet of wild blackberries.

⑪ Recycled glass homeware Stylish and ethical wine glasses, jugs and decanters made from recycled glass are the height of eco design.

⑫ Membership of an environmental organization There are many worthwhile groups promoting a more sustainable way of life.

⑬ Charitable gift From tree seedlings to health & hygiene kits, a donation to a charity will help provide basic necessities to those who need it in the developing world – and is a perfect gift for someone who has everything.

⑭ Home-made liqueur Take a bottle of gin, vodka or whisky and add your choice of fruit; sloe gin or raspberry vodka make wonderfully delicious gifts.

⑮ Organic bodycare products The skin absorbs most of what we put on it, so opt for organic essential oils, herbs and other natural ingredients when giving a pampering bodycare present.

⑯ A cloth nappy set Easy to use, and better for a baby and the environment; help a new parent make a dent in the tonnes of nappy waste going to landfill with a set of reusables.

⑰ Promised deeds Anything from gardening help, childcare or a candlelit meal, an "IOU" can be tailored specifically to the recipient.

⑱ Reusable carrier bag Help someone get over a plastic bag addiction with a handy, long-lasting carrier bag made from cotton, linen or hemp.

⑲ Books promoting sustainable activities These could include guides for cycling, walking, camping or any and all types of flora and fauna.

⑳ Eco kitchen kettle An environmentally friendly kettle that ensures that you only boil the amount of water you actually need – saving water, energy and time.

WEAR & SLEEP IN NATURAL ORGANIC FABRICS

Why wear natural organic fabrics like cotton, wool, linen and hemp? Natural fibres allow the skin to breathe more easily than most synthetic fibres, and have a less harmful impact on the environment.

We all wear and decorate our homes with many different fabrics. As well as looking good, fabrics have to be soft against the skin, robust enough to be tugged or sat on, warm, waterproof, washable, crease-resistant or just plain comfy. With all these demands, it is little wonder that we rarely stop to think about what our clothes are actually made of and how textiles might be affecting our health or the environment.

The night clothes and bedsheets you sleep in probably spend more time in contact with your skin than anything in your wardrobe. As you sweat at night, your skin becomes moist, allowing some of the chemicals that may be on a fabric to be more easily absorbed by your skin. So you may want to think most about these fabrics.

Four good things about natural fibres

■ Natural fibres wick water and sweat away from the skin, so they are more breathable than synthetic fibres.

■ Natural fabrics are usually easier to dye than synthetic ones, so fewer chemicals are needed to manufacture them.

■ Natural fibres will rot away. You can even put discarded clothes on a compost heap.

■ Natural fibres are made from renewable resources that can be re-grown. Synthetics are made from oil, which cannot be replaced once it has been used.

Buy organic fabrics

Don't just assume that if your textiles are natural, they are good for the environment. Even natural textiles, or rather the way they are grown, can be extremely damaging. Many of these problems are avoided with organically produced fabrics:

■ Cotton is the most heavily sprayed crop on earth. It is responsible for over ten per cent of all pesticides sold, causing poisonings, water contamination and soil damage all around the world.

■ Cotton has been genetically modified to tolerate herbicides or to resist insect pests. In the USA, over three quarters of the cotton crop is GM. In theory, cotton engineered to make its own pesticides should need fewer chemical sprays. However, different insect pests are taking over and the main cotton pests are becoming resistant to the GM cotton, meaning that farmers still have to spray their crops just as often.

Natural organic cotton clothes, bed clothes, baby clothes and towels cause less harm to the environment, and you and your children will be exposed to fewer potentially harmful chemicals from fabric treatments and finishes.

Manufacturing processes

Most fibres go through some chemical processing before being sold as clothing. These include:

● Dyeing and bleaching
Many dyes have been linked to allergies. The worst are those used on synthetic fabrics.

● Chemical treatments
Easy-care fabrics, for example, are treated using a process that releases formaldehyde and ammonia. Treated fabrics can cause contact dermititis in susceptible people.

● Plasticized printing
Plastic designs printed onto fabric can contain very high levels of phthalates – chemicals that have a hormonal effect and are potentially carcinogenic. Children who chew and suck their clothing may ingest these compounds.

● Insecticides and fungicides
These are sometimes used on fabrics while they are being stored in warehouses.

Shopping tips

You can help to combat many of the worst social, environmental and health problems caused by the textile industry by shopping wisely:

Buy organic fibres whenever possible.

Buy alternative natural fibres Linen, hemp, wool and silk are all better for the environment than non-organically produced materials.

Avoid cheap clothing The true cost of a £3 T-shirt is probably abusive labour practices and environmentally harmful production methods.

Buy second-hand clothes in charity shops.

Look for fleeces and other clothing made from recycled plastics.

Avoid "disposable fashion" Invest in better-made, more durable items of clothing that won't end up in a landfill site after being worn only a few times.

After you've bought new clothes and fabrics, wash them first before using them to rinse out many of the processing and storage chemicals that might otherwise end up in contact with your skin. Avoid dry-cleaning clothes, as the solvents used damage the environment.

Fibre guide

Natural fibres These fibres come directly from plants or animals. They include wool, cotton, linen, hemp and silk (from the cocoons of silkmoth caterpillars that feed on mulberry leaves).

Semi-synthetic The raw ingredient for viscose (rayon) and acetate is cellulose, made from wood chips. Cellulose fibres are found in all plants, and make up the bulk of wood. The cellulose is dissolved using chemical processes, then the mixture is squeezed through a spinneret, which has many small holes, to make fine filaments.

Synthetic fibres The raw ingredients for synthetic fibres are produced by the petrochemical industry from crude oil. They include nylon, acrylic and polyester. The most common type of polyester is also used for packaging, and plastic bottles can be recycled to make clothing. PVC (polyvinyl chloride) is used for many products, including clothing. Making and disposing of PVC creates and releases dioxin, one of the most toxic chemicals there is.

GO GREEN IN THE PLAYROOM

The toys you purchase can have a positive influence, not just on the workers or the environment where the toys are made, but also on the imagination and creativity of your children. It just takes a little thought about where a toy is from, how it was made, what it is made of, and how a child could use it.

Avoid harmful chemicals

Children are particularly vulnerable to the effects of chemical exposure, as they go through so many developmental changes. Young children suck or chew anything within their reach, so it makes sense to avoid toys and equipment that contain harmful chemicals.

■ Buy toys made from natural products such as wood, cotton, hemp and wool.

■ Choose toys that use non-toxic dyes, paints and natural oil finishes such as linseed and beeswax.

■ Avoid soft plastic toys. Many contain plasticizers called phthalates that are known to be harmful. These have been banned from toys in many countries, but can still be found in clothing with plastic designs, pram covers and so on.

Fair play

Choosing toys that have been made according to ethical standards, such as those of the Fairtrade Foundation, ensures that workers get fair wages and that there has been no abuse of child labour.

■ Avoid toys produced by global brands unless you are sure of their employment practices.

■ Think local: buy from local craftspeople or community-based toy-making groups if possible.

Stay green by reusing toys

One of the greenest things you can do is to avoid buying new toys.

● Exchange toys with friends.

● Use toy-swap schemes.

● Sell and buy used toys via the internet or local papers.

● Invent "alternative" toys. A cardboard box and a wooden spoon can provide hours of entertainment for very young children.

● Make your own. For example, try making your own modelling dough using flour and vegetable oil.

You could also:

● Write to toy manufacturers asking about their policies on employment practices: 75% of all toys are made in China, where millions of workers have to work long hours for low pay, often in dangerous conditions.

FORAGE FOR FUNGI

If you have ever been lucky enough to pick a basket of field mushrooms and bring them home to eat, you will know that nothing beats the intensity of their flavour and the wonderful aroma that they give off. Learn to find and identify the right mushrooms for the most delicious harvest.

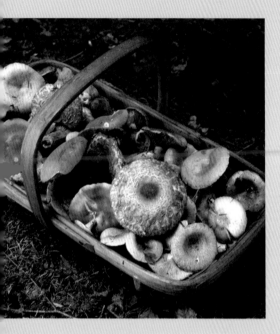

It's not usual to be able to pick field mushrooms all year round, but you can forage for a wide variety of fungi for several months – mainly in late summer and autumn, and also in spring and even in winter for a few species such as velvet shank (*Flammulina velutipes*). Wild fungi will not grow where chemical fertilizers or sprays have been used, so not only are your pickings free, you can be sure that they are pesticide-free too.

If you are a beginner, start by joining a guided fungi foray or a fungi course, or by teaming up with an experienced forager. This will help you to know where to look, to tell the difference between various species and to recognise what stage of growth the mushrooms are at.

Fungi do not use energy from the sun, as plants do, to make their food. Instead, they absorb food and water from their surroundings. The edible parts are the fruiting bodies, which change in appearance according to the weather and as they mature. They grow in a wide variety of environments, but the best places to look for them are woodlands (especially clearings or the edges of woodlands), old pastures where horses or cattle have grazed, and grassland.

Although correct identification is the first step in safe harvesting, you also need to pay attention to the condition of a mushroom. An overripe or decomposing mushroom can cause digestive upsets, and some people react with skin rashes to certain edible species.

On the menu

There are about 100 mushrooms that are known to be edible. Some of these are so prized – such as the Cep and Chanterelle – that seasoned fungi hunters try to keep their locations a secret. Here is a selection of the best varieties.

Parasol
(Lepiota procera)
Scaly brown/grey cap that opens like an umbrella. Remove stem before cooking. Grows in clearings and gardens.

Morel
(Morchella esculenta)
Pitted brownish cap. Must be cooked. Appears in spring in woodlands, clearings and in hedgerows.

Shaggy ink cap
(Coprinus comatus)
White, scaly fungus. Gills change from white to pink, brown, then black. Grows in grassy places.

Giant puffball
(Langermannia gigantean)
White, ball-shaped. Pick when young before flesh turns yellow. Grows in meadows, pastures and under hedges.

Chanterelle
(Cantharellus cibarius)
Yellow wavy-edged cap and stalk. Grows in woodland clearings.

Bay boletus
(Boletus badius)
Pale to chestnut brown cap with yellow pores on the underside. Pick when young. Grows in woods.

Cep
(Boletus edulis)
Brownish, bun-shaped cap. Bulbous stalk. Check cap for insects before eating. Grows in woodlands and hedgerows.

Field mushroom
(Agaricus campestris)
Whitish cap with pink gills and a thin ring round the stem. Grows in pastures and meadows.

Off the menu

Some mushrooms are poisonous, a few of which are identified below, and the effects can vary from a stomach upset to severe, or even fatal, liver damage. The Shaggy parasol (*Macrolepiota rhacodes*) (*right*) can cause stomach upsets.

Fly agaric
(Amanita muscaria)
Scarlet with white patches, which fade as it matures.

Death cap
(Amanita phalloides)
Distinctive white gills with a sheath at the base of the stalk.

Yellow stainer
(Agaricus xanthodermus)
The white cap turns greyish with age. Flesh is bright yellow.

Woolly milk cap
(Lactarius torminosus)
Woolly-looking cap that forms a depression in the middle.

Foraging the green way

In some areas fungi are becoming scarce, either as a result of over-collecting or because the habitat where they grow has altered or been destroyed. Try to follow these few simple rules to make sure that more fungi will emerge the following season in the places where you have been foraging.

■ Collect no more than half the fungi present, or a maximum of 1.5kg (3lb 5oz) in weight.

■ Only take as many fungi as you can use.

■ Pick by twisting the stalk, not by cutting, which can damage the network of threads left in the ground.

■ If you are a beginner, go with an experienced forager or take a reliable field guide with you so that you only pick fungi that you can eat.

Foraging tips

● Don't pick on wet days.

● Don't pick decaying fungi.

● Use a basket, not a polythene bag, to bring home your fungi, as they decay quickly in warm, stale air.

● Use mushrooms within 24 hours of picking them.

● Before cooking, cut each fungus in half and throw away any that show signs of maggots, or have white gills.

● Only eat a small amount if the species is new to you in case it disagrees with you.

Mushroom frittata

(serves 2)

This is a simple yet delicious way of cooking wild mushrooms. If you can't go foraging, or wild fungi aren't in season, use chestnut mushrooms, which have a good, meaty flavour.

Ingredients

25g (1oz) butter

85g (3oz) wild or chestnut mushrooms, sliced

1 shallot, finely chopped

1 clove garlic, finely chopped

4 eggs

1 teaspoon fresh thyme, finely chopped

Salt and pepper to taste

A few leaves of fresh basil as a garnish (optional)

Method

■ Melt the butter in a frying pan and cook the mushrooms, shallot and garlic until they are soft and beginning to take on some colour.

■ Beat the eggs with the thyme, salt and pepper.

■ Pour the egg mixture over the mushrooms and cook gently over a medium heat until set.

■ Slide under a grill to brown the top, then scatter over the basil leaves if you wish and serve hot or cold.

CHOOSE SAFE PRODUCTS FOR CHILDREN

You may think of your skin as a barrier, but in reality it is more like a sponge. It can absorb up to 60 per cent of whatever you put on it. Children's skins are particularly vulnerable to the chemicals in bath products and in the environment.

Children differ from adults in a number of ways that can increase their susceptibility to toxins in the home. For example:

■ Children's skin is thinner and more absorbent than that of adults, thus providing a less effective barrier to environmental toxins.

■ Their immune systems are less able to defend against poisons and allergens.

■ They eat, drink and breathe in more for their weight than adults, and so take in more toxins per kilogram. Even at rest, an infant will breath in twice the volume of air as an adult.

■ Crawling on the floor and putting objects in their mouths means that young children come into contact with dust and other potentially toxic particles.

Shampoos, body washes and moisturisers are all easily absorbed through the scalp and skin, so avoid using products that contain synthetic perfumes, colours and preservatives on your children's skin. You should also avoid using harsh detergents and cleaning products, which can contaminate the air and surfaces in the home.

Checklist for children

Buy fragrance-free, organic bath products (soaps, shampoos, body washes).

Choose plant-based, gentle organic skincare products (oils, creams, toothpaste).

Treat babies' skins with the utmost care. Buy fragrance- and chemical-free baby wipes, nappy cream, and washable or biodegradable nappies.

Read and understand the label. Avoid cleaning products (disinfectants, bleaches, aerosols, carpet cleaners) that contain harmful chemicals.

A dry skin solution

Using harsh toiletries on sensitive skin may be a contributing factor to the rising rate of eczema and allergies among children. Although parents whose children have skin rashes often approach the problem by applying more products to the skin, cutting out baby toiletries altogether could be a more effective solution.

If your child has dry or irritated skin, try making your own herbal wash bag.

Cut the foot off an old pair of tights, about 15cm (6in) from the end, to use as a pouch.

Fill the pouch with a handful of oatmeal and, if you wish, some soothing herbs such as chamomile or lavender.

Tie a knot in the open end of the pouch.

Use in the bath or shower. One wash bag will last one day maximum – keep it in the fridge in a plastic bag if you intend to use it morning and night, but don't try to store it for longer, as it can accumulate bacteria. When wet it will produce a lovely creamy liquid that will clean and nourish skin without drying it. Great for babies and children, but also good for adults.

2 ROOF TERRACE, PATIO OR TINY GARDEN

GROW BEANS ON A WIGWAM

If you want to grow vegetables that will crop over many weeks and also make an attractive, leafy screen on your patio or balcony, plant some climbing beans. They don't take up much ground space, and the more you pick the tender, crunchy beans, the more the plants produce. The flowers on bean plants are so striking – scarlet, white, pink or bicoloured – that garden designers often include them for their decorative value in their designs.

Beans need to grow in well-fertilized soil that is rich in compost. Runner beans *(Phaseolus coccineus)* and the finer French beans *(Phaseolus vulgaris)*, also called pole beans or haricot vert, will need some kind of support to help them climb, and wigwams are the best – and prettiest – option. If you don't have space for a wigwam, grow a dwarf type of bean that doesn't need support, such as runner beans 'Pickwick' and 'Hestia', or French beans 'The Prince' and 'Annabel'.

Growing beans from seed

Both kinds of bean need a sheltered, sunny spot. The soil needs to be a minimum temperature of 10°C (50°F) for the seeds to germinate.

The seeds will get off to a quicker start if you sow them indoors, one seed per pot, at a depth of 4cm (1½in).

Water the pots well, put on a sunny windowsill and don't let the compost dry out.

If you are sowing outdoors, it's best to warm the soil first for French beans by covering it with polythene or fleece for a couple of weeks before sowing. Seedlings sown indoors should be ready to plant out in about three weeks, but make sure you put them outside for a few days beforehand to harden them off.

Planting bean seedlings

■ The container you choose should be at least 45cm (18in) in diameter, with drainage holes and a layer of crocks at the bottom.

■ Fill the container with a mixture of equal parts loam-based compost and loam-free compost.

■ Before planting the seedlings, fix the wigwam in place. You can buy a wigwam to fit the size of the pot, or make your own using four or five 2m (6ft) tall bamboo canes. Push the canes into the earth around the edge of the container until they touch the bottom of the pot. Gather the tops of the canes together and secure them with string to form a wigwam shape.

■ Plant out the seedlings, one by each cane. French beans are not hardy and should be planted outside only when all risk of frost has passed. Tie the seedlings onto the canes as they climb. When each plant reaches the top of its support, pinch out the tips to encourage bushier, more productive growth lower down.

■ Keep the containers well watered (French beans can tolerate hotter, drier conditions) and feed the plants with a liquid fertilizer if they need a boost.

■ Start harvesting from midsummer for tender young beans, snipping them off with a pair of scissors. Both runner beans and French beans freeze well if you have a glut.

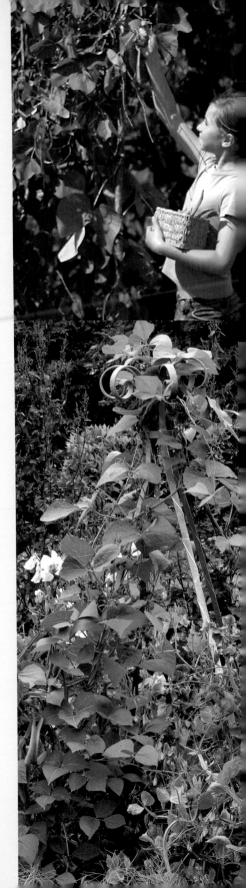

Grow potatoes in a tub

Grow a crop of delicious potatoes by planting them in a container or barrel. You can make your own using a wooden barrel, a deep plastic pot (look for a recycled range) at least 30cm (12in) in diameter, or even an old dustbin.

■ Make sure that your container is positioned in a light spot, and has drainage holes and a layer of crocks at the bottom.

■ Use well-chitted (sprouted) seed potatoes and choose fast-growing early varieties (planted in early spring) and second earlies (about a month later).

■ Fill the container with a 10–12.5cm (4–5in) layer of good multi-purpose compost and stand the potatoes on top of the soil, with the sprouts facing upwards and positioned about 18cm (7in) apart. A pot that is 30–40cm (12–16in) in diameter and about 40cm (16in) deep will accommodate a maximum of two seed potatoes.

■ Water the soil well, and when the potato shoots are about 15cm (6in) tall, cover them with another layer of compost so that the tips of the plants are just showing. Continue to build up the earth in this way until the shoots are just below the rim of the container.

■ Keep the container well watered, especially if the weather is hot. Once the pretty flowers have appeared, feed weekly with a liquid organic feed, such as comfrey.

■ In early summer, check on the size of the potatoes by scraping away some of the compost around them.

■ Once the potatoes are about the size of a hen's egg, you can dig them out and prepare a dish of your own nutritious and tasty home-grown new potatoes.

KEEP URBAN HONEY BEES

Bees are an important part of an organic eco-system, but you don't need to own a rural retreat in order to keep bees and harvest their honey: a small garden, or even a rooftop terrace, is a perfect place for a beehive – all you need is a flat outdoor space.

Urban beekeepers have the advantage that cities tend to be warmer than rural areas, so the bees are more active and their season for foraging for nectar is longer. And with a far greater selection of plants on display in highly planted parks, gardens and windowboxes there's usually something in flower all year round. This means that urban bees have the potential to produce a richer variety of honey and higher yields.

Bees prefer to have a clear flight path upwards out of the hive, which should face south if possible. From an urban beekeeper's point of view, it's also worth keeping the hive in a secluded place to avoid people being stung. If you have a garden without a high wall, plant tall shrubs or hedges or erect a fence to encourage the bees' flight path up and over peoples' heads. Once they are up in the air, the bees go in various directions to forage.

Getting started

There are many local beekeeping societies and groups who will be happy to help in providing advice, equipment, and the bees to get you started.

Beneficial properties of honey

- Honey contains vitamins and antioxidants, and enzymes that help in its digestion.
- It's an excellent natural preservative.
- Honey has been used in healing remedies for at least 4,000 years. It is now known to act as an antiseptic/antibacterial agent, and is most commonly used as an anti-microbial agent used for dressing wounds, burns and skin ulcers.

PLANT BLUEBERRY BUSHES

There are many good reasons for growing your own blueberries: they are delicious to eat, either fresh or in pies; they are a "superfood" containing high levels of antioxidants that have anti-ageing benefits, help to keep your eyes healthy and can protect against cancer; and they make delightful garden plants, with scented flowers in spring, dusty-blue fruits and brilliant autumn foliage. Once you get a taste for blueberries, you'll want to eat a handful every day; picking your own bush-ripened berries means they'll always be at their freshest.

Until recently, it was thought that blueberries could only be grown in large beds of acidic soil. Now we know that they can thrive in containers, given the right conditions, and that the soil in these pots doesn't have to be 100 per-cent ericaceous (acid) compost. In fact, specialist growers are now recommending that the compost for blueberries in containers consists of at least 50 per-cent fine-composted pine or fir bark, which helps to acidify the soil. If you prefer to garden peat-free (most ericaceous compost contains peat), you could try a 100 per-cent mixture of fine- and medium-grade bark chippings, with some perlite added to help retain moisture. Most blueberries need another blueberry plant of a different variety for pollination, so check with your local grower or garden centre before buying your plants.

Why garden peat-free?

Peatlands are a precious habitat in the same way that rainforests are. A community of insects, animals and plants, some of them unique to peatlands, depend on the watery layers of decayed plants that build up over thousands of years to form peat. Peatlands also absorb and store CO_2 from the atmosphere – when they are drained and peat is extracted for fuel or horticulture, this carbon is released, adding to global warming.

One of the greatest threats to peat bogs is gardening, as most bagged multi-purpose composts are peat-based. Peat has become a mainstay of these composts because it is consistent, sterile and low in nutrients. But when peat becomes waterlogged it forms a solid mass that plant roots find hard to penetrate, and it has no benefit as a soil conditioner or a mulch. In recent years, non-peat composts, based on coir, composted wood, bark and green waste and other natural materials, have become widely available.

What you can do

● Buy compost bags labelled "peat-free" or "peat-reduced".

● Make your own compost and use it as a mulch and soil conditioner.

Blueberries in pots need

■ A free-draining acidic soil.

■ Moisture throughout the growing season, although the pots should not be waterlogged.

■ A top dressing in spring with a slow-release fertilizer.

■ Pruning in winter: cut out any spindly or damaged stems and, once the bush is three years old, cut one or two of the oldest stems down to ground level to encourage new shoots to grow.

■ Pick the fruit when they are fully blue and ripe.

For successful crops

■ Make sure that the composted bark you use is untreated.

■ Take off all but about five or six flowers in the first year of growth so that the plants become well established before they put their energy into fruiting.

■ Use rainwater if possible, although tap water is better than not watering at all.

■ Don't use animal manure or animal-based fertilizers, or tomato feed.

Good blueberry varieties to grow

Northern highbush (varieties of *Vaccinium corymbosum*) can grow to 2m (6ft) tall in the ground, but will be more compact in containers.

'Duke' grows to about 1.5m (5ft) and crops in mid-summer.

'Bluecrop' produces good crops of large berries in late summer.

Herbert is one of the best varieties for flavour, and has bright red autumn foliage. Fruits ripen in late summer.

Half-high blueberries (hybrids between *Vaccinium angustifolium* and *V corymbosum*) are hardy and more compact, growing to about 1.5m (5ft).

'Northblue' produces its large berries in early summer.

Most southern highbush blueberries (complex hybrids) are evergreen and cannot survive very cold winter temperatures.

'Sunshine Blue' is compact, has an excellent flavour and can tolerate less acidic soils.

Blueberry muffins

Ingredients

140g (5oz) wholemeal flour

140g (5oz) plain flour

2 teaspoons baking powder

1 teaspoon baking soda

50g (2oz) butter

50g (2oz) honey

85g (3oz) fresh or 50g (2oz) dried blueberries

1 egg, lightly beaten

275g (10oz) natural yoghurt

Method

■ Preheat the oven to 180°C/350°F/Gas 4.

■ Mix the flours, baking powder and soda together in a bowl. Make a well in the centre.

■ Gently melt the butter and honey in a pan, pour into the well with the blueberries, egg and yoghurt and very gently mix into the flour, allowing the mixture to remain slightly lumpy. Don't over-mix or the muffins will be heavy.

■ Spoon the mixture into muffin tins lined with muffin cases. Bake for 20 minutes or until the tops are light brown.

Variation
Cranberry & orange muffins

Replace the blueberries with 50g (2oz) dried cranberries and the grated zest of 2 oranges.

GROW AN APPLE TREE IN A POT

You don't have to own acres of garden to grow your own apples. All you need is the right kind of apple tree, compost and a pot. Then, as long as you remember to water and feed it, you should get showers of pretty blossom in spring, followed by your own crop of juicy apples in autumn.

Buying the right kind of apple is important, so it's a good idea to get help from a fruit nursery. Apples are grown on a range of different rootstocks (the plant that provides the root system), depending on the size and form of the tree required. For pot-grown apples, the best rootstock is M26, which will produce dwarf trees either as bushes, cordons (single-stemmed, usually grown at an oblique angle) or minarettes (single-stemmed, column-shaped). Decide what shape you want – minarettes are ideal if you're really tight for space – and whether you want more than one tree. If you only have room for one, choose a self-fertile apple such as Falstaff, Greensleeves, Fiesta or Red Windsor. If you buy two or more apple trees, make sure they are from the same pollination group, and look for disease-resistant varieties that crop well. Your supplier should be able to advise you.

Three easy steps

■ Plant a one-year-old tree (also called a maiden) in late autumn in a pot about 30–38cm (12–15in) in diameter. Put a layer of crocks at the bottom for drainage and fill with a loam-based compost. Place in a sheltered spot out of the prevailing wind. Increase the watering in spring and give it liquid feeds.

■ Prune your tree to shape it and make a good framework of branches that will bear plenty of fruit. Ask for pruning instructions when you buy the plant.

■ Repot your tree into a larger pot every year until it is fully grown. After that, prune the roots every three years or so and re-fill the pot with fresh compost.

Tips on growing an apple tree

Stand the pot on bricks to help with drainage.

In winter, water sparingly, making sure that the compost does not dry out completely. Move the pot to a sheltered spot out of the prevailing wind. If a heavy frost is expected, wrap the pot in sacking or horticultural fleece

In spring, increase watering and start feeding with a high-potash liquid feed such as tomato feed.

In midsummer the pot may need watering twice a day. Feed every 7–10 days.

You can grow other fruits in pots too – pears, peaches, nectarines, apricots and figs – but these plants need more attention and extra protection.

START A WORMERY

Nearly 40 per cent of our domestic refuse is organic material – things like vegetable and fruit peelings, tea bags and food scraps – which can and should be recycled. If they're sent to landfill sites, they produce methane, a potent greenhouse gas that contributes to global warming, and a liquid called leachate, which can contaminate water supplies.

An excellent way of being environmentally responsible and recycling your own organic waste is to feed it to a colony of worms in a wormery. These obliging wrigglers devour the waste (each worm eats up to half its bodyweight every day) in a dark bin and produce two natural byproducts: a top quality compost that gardeners sometimes call "Black Gold", which you can use to condition the soil in your garden and in containers; and a liquid that you can dilute to make a superb tonic for your plants.

You can make your own wormery, using stackable storage boxes, wire mesh, a drain cock and synthetic carpet for a lid, but the simplest way to get started is to buy a readymade kit, complete with a supply of the same kind of worms that normally live in well-rotted manure or compost heaps.

Indoors or outdoors?

Wormery bins are often described as "odour free", but many people find that when they lift the lid off to add more scraps, a strong earthy smell wafts out. So, it may be a better idea to keep your wormery in a utility room or outside the back door, rather than in the kitchen. Even if you rather like the earthy smell, you may find that the liquid that you need to siphon off too pungent. When draining off this liquid, use rubber gloves and store the concentrated plant food in a jar with a tight lid until you need to use it. Then dilute it 1:10 with water and watch your plants perk up within days.

Another reason for keeping the bin outside is that fruit flies are often attracted to the waste in summer and lay their eggs in it. They're harmless, but a nuisance in the kitchen.

What composting worms like

■ A mixture of dry and wet waste, such as vegetable scraps, fruit peelings and cores, egg shells, coffee grains, tea bags, cardboard from eggboxes and toilet roll centres, shredded paper, dust from the vacuum cleaner.

■ Dark, moist (but not wet) living conditions, at a fairly constant temperature. Keep them out of scorching heat in summer, and protected from frost during winter (for example, with an insulation jacket).

■ Good air circulation.

■ Regular amounts of waste, chopped up small or shredded.

What composting worms don't like

■ Too thick a layer of waste above them, which cuts off their air supply and makes their living conditions sour and airless.

■ Too many foods that make the conditions acid, such as onions and lemons.

■ Waterlogged living conditions – the liquid at the bottom needs to be drained off frequently and dry waste, especially cardboard, needs to be added regularly.

How it works

The wormery is a bin (usually plastic) with a lid, and layers or chambers through which the worms move as they eat up the waste.

There is a collector tray at the bottom which holds the liquid that is produced, with a tap to run it off. The lowest chamber has a layer of bedding where the worms live to start with.

As you add small amounts of waste, the worms wriggle up the chambers to eat it – they can eat at least half their own weight in a day – and their casts (droppings) sink down.

Once almost full, take out of the bin the "Black Gold" in the bottom chamber and start again. If you provide the right conditions and regularly siphon off the liquid, the worms will go on eating and breeding for years on end.

USE ECO-FRIENDLY DIY MATERIALS

Whether you are considering a building project, painting a room or just adding new furnishings to your home, there are plenty of ways in which you can lower your impact on the environment and minimize your exposure to potentially hazardous substances.

Reusing materials rather than buying new is always the most environmentally responsible option. So-called "environmental" materials are not actually good for the environment; they are just less damaging than non-environmental materials. It's better to reuse salvaged rainforest hardwoods from a demolished building, for example, than to buy new "ethical" wood. And recycled plastics may be an appropriate choice, even if you normally avoid using plastic.

Try some of these ideas to help you feel good about, and not be made ill by, the materials that surround you in your home.

Choose the right materials

Many of the products recommended for DIY projects contain very unpleasant chemicals. Check the labels for hazard or health warnings before you buy, and try to source safer alternatives. There are a whole range of natural, responsibly sourced choices if you decide to buy new materials.

Avoid if possible

Polyvinyl Chloride (PVC) is widely used as a construction material for products such as cables, pipes, flooring and panelling. The production and disposal of PVC creates and releases toxic chemicals into the environment.

Medium Density Fibreboard (MDF) contains urea formaldehyde. The dust generated from cutting or sanding MDF is dangerous, and low levels of the chemical can be released throughout the life of the product.

Timber treatments Many timber treatments are toxic to humans, pets and wildlife.

Fungicides Many wallpaper pastes contain fungicides.

Harmful solvents Paint strippers, paint thinners, varnish removers and brush cleaners usually contain very strong and potentially harmful solvents.

Formaldehydes Floor sealants can contain formaldehydes and other harmful chemicals.

Aluminium is very energy-intensive to produce. Use alternatives, such as wood for window frames.

Wood materials

Choose wood that is sustainably harvested and, if possible, from a local source to reduce the impact of transport.

Timber certified by the Forestry Stewardship Council (FSC) guarantees that your wood is from a well-managed forest that meets strict environmental, social and economic standards.

Many wood treatments are toxic to human beings, pets and wildlife. Ask suppliers what has been used to treat the wood before you buy it.

Chipboard and MDF tend to be made of waste wood, but the adhesives used to glue the particles together can contain formaldehyde and other unpleasant chemicals.

Consider using recycled plastic "wood" for floors, fences, play equipment and garden furniture. It prevents plastic drink bottles going into landfill and can even be recycled again.

VOCs in paints

A major hazard in paints and varnishes is VOCs – Volatile Organic Compounds. In this case the word "organic" is used in the chemical sense, meaning that the compounds contain carbon. "Volatile" means that they evaporate readily at typical room temperatures. If the chemicals are also harmful, it means that they have a high potential for causing health problems because they can easily enter the body. Most paints now carry VOC ratings. Also, not all VOCs are harmful or synthetic. Alcohol and citrus oils are classed as VOCs.

Paints & finishes

Ordinary paints are manufactured from complex synthetic chemicals, some of which can be damaging to health. Natural paints are made using ingredients close to their natural state.

Headaches and allergies are common side effects of decorating and, according to the World Health Organization, professional painters and decorators face a 40 per-cent higher than average risk of lung cancer. Paint manufacture is also harmful to the environment. Making one tonne of ordinary paint results in 10 tonnes of waste, much of it toxic. Petrochemical solvent-based ("oil-based") paints

Make milk paint

Mix 250g (½lb) casein powder with 340ml (12fl oz) water. Whisk to a thick batter. Stand for 30 minutes.

Add another 125ml (4fl oz) of water. Whisk to a creamy consistency. Leave to stand for 15 minutes more.

Mix 50g (2oz) of pigment powder with a little water to make a thin paste. Add the casein mix, stir and use.

are recognized as being harmful, so many paint manufacturers have developed water-based alternatives. Although lower in smelly solvents (VOCs), water-based paints can contain even more harmful chemicals, and require complex and energy-intensive manufacturing processes.

Choose natural paints

■ The components in natural paint are based on plant oils and extracts such as linseed oil, citrus oils, balsamic turpentine and simple minerals. They involve less intensive processing, which uses less energy and produces less waste.

■ Natural paints can also be better for your home surfaces. They are slightly porous, so they tend to allow plaster to "breathe" – unlike most conventional paints, which tend to seal surfaces.

■ Natural paints may cost more than mass-produced petrochemical alternatives, but the hidden costs to your health will be much less.

■ Many natural paints and finishes are widely available. Larger DIY stores often sell natural products and many companies sell via the internet or by mail order.

■ Alternatively, make your own paint. Casein powder, a by-product of milk, can be mixed with water and a small amount of pigment to make a smooth, matt "milk paint" for interior walls.

Floorings

Cover your floors with material that is attractive, practical, durable and environmentally sound: most carpets contain synthetic dyes and a heavy mix of chemicals, so choose natural alternatives instead.

Wool is one of the best materials for carpets. It is hard-wearing and naturally flame-resistant. Although wool carpets tend to be more expensive, if properly cared for they can last for 50 years or more. Use cork or wool for the underlay. Recycled underlays made from old car tyres, fibre scraps or compressed wood fibres are also available.

Grass rugs or carpets made of sisal, coir or seagrass are another natural flooring alternative.

Solid timber flooring is a good, natural choice, but check that the wood is sustainably harvested and locally sourced if possible.

Existing wooden floors can often be sanded and used again. If not, consider using reclaimed floorboards.

Floor tiles can be made out of natural materials such as clay or stone. However, consider the extraction and transport implications.

Cork flooring is sourced from the bark of Cork oak trees. Mediterranean Cork oak forests are harvested sustainably. These forests need all the help they can get – they are less profitable now that many wines are sold with plastic corks.

Natural linoleum (not its PVC imitation) is made from linseed oil and other natural ingredients.

Planning a building project?

Does it need doing, and do you need to do as much as you think? Major projects involve a lot of work, create a large amount of waste, and require many new materials.

Plan around what is available by designing around fittings and other items that you can salvage. For example, rather than rip out a whole kitchen, just change the cupboard doors to update the look.

Plan for recycling: by using nails and screws rather than glue, items will be easier to dismantle in the future and so be more easily reused or recycled.

Try to reuse old bricks.

Assess quantities of paint and other materials to avoid waste.

Think long-term: cheap materials and poor workmanship are likely to need replacing or redoing in a year or two's time, creating more waste. If you budget for the likely cost over decades, rather than the immediate cost of a job, materials that seem expensive may actually save you money.

Extraction and transport of stone and aggregates can cause environmental problems. Ask your supplier or builder's merchant where products have been quarried or obtained.

Cement production is an energy-intensive industry producing vast quantities of carbon dioxide. In fact, cement manufacturing is the third largest cause of man-made carbon dioxide emissions. Consider using lime mortar as an alternative.

Using contractors? Look for websites listing environmentally aware builders and architects.

Decorating a child's bedroom?

Create safe, healthy surroundings that don't cost the earth.

- Use natural paints.
- Use natural flooring materials.
- Avoid wall-to-wall carpets that can house dust-mites.
- If you are stripping very old paint, check for lead content. Avoid plastics and PVC; use untreated wood and natural fabrics on cots and other nursery furniture.
- If you are pregnant, be especially careful to avoid potentially toxic ingredients (for example, MDF, which contains formaldehyde). If a label says "danger", "warning" or "caution", ask the retailer for the product's safety data sheet. This will explain the specific hazards involved and how to deal with them. Some ingredients, such as strong acids or strong alkalis, may burn or blind if splashed onto the skin or eyes, but they have no long-term effects on the unborn baby.

TRAIN A FIG TREE AGAINST A WALL

It's no wonder figs were a staple food in Ancient Greece and Rome. They thrive in warm, sunny climates where they produce fruit two or three times a year; they are sweet and succulent; and they are packed full of easily digested nutrients. Because they are soft-skinned, they do not travel well and so are best eaten, fully ripe, straight from the tree.

If you have a warm, sheltered wall facing south or south west, you can grow figs outdoors in a temperate climate. Under glass, with a minimum temperature of 13°C (55°F) from January onwards, you should be able to get two crops; outdoors, only one will ripen, even though the tree may form a second crop.

How to grow figs

The best way to grow a fig against a wall is to train it in a fan shape. This provides a lovely covering of big leaves, but for edible fruit you must give the plant special attention.

■ Restrict the roots to keep the tree compact and make it bear fruit – if you don't, the strong roots will romp away through the soil and all you'll get is leaves. You can do this in two ways: by planting the tree in a pot that has good drainage and is at least 45cm (18in) in diameter, and sinking it into the ground; or by making a "box" or pit at least 60cm (24in) deep, lined with concrete or overlapping paving slabs and with a thick layer of bricks or rubble in the bottom. Both pot and box should be filled with soil-based compost, with pieces of brick or large grit added.

■ Attach vine eyes 20cm (8in) apart, starting at 35cm (14in) from the ground, up the wall, and fix horizontal wires to them. Also ensure the wires are 5–10cm (2–4in) away from the wall to allow for air circulation when the plant is tied onto them.

■ Plant the tree 20cm (8in) away from the wall. As the tree grows, tie the side shoots to the wires to form a fan shape.

■ Water the tree frequently in the summer, daily if it's very dry, or the developing fruit will drop off.

■ The tiny fruits that form towards the end of the summer need to be protected in winter in cold areas. Cover them with bracken or straw held in place by mesh netting.

■ The fig should be pruned in early spring, and any large fruits on the branches taken off.

What to plant

There are many varieties of fig, some with brown or purple skin and reddish flesh, others with yellowish-green skin and pale flesh.

Brown Turkey The best cropper for UK patios and gardens.

Brunswick has larger fruits and ripens a couple of weeks earlier than Brown Turkey.

Bourjasotte Grise is especially sweet and needs to be grown under glass, or in a pot and brought indoors in winter.

You can expect some fruit the first year after planting. Once the tree is carrying a heavy crop, feed with a high potash liquid feed until the figs ripen.

MAKE YOUR OWN BARBECUE

Treat yourself to a green barbecue of delicious foods. Recycle a spare terracotta pot from the garden instead of buying an expensive high-tech metal barbecue, and use charcoal from sustainably managed woodlands.

More than 90 per cent of our barbecue charcoal is imported, and much of it is likely to come from unsustainably managed tropical forests. By buying charcoal made from trees that have been coppiced (when trees and shrubs are trimmed back to produce a supply of thin poles) and thinned in woodlands, you are using sustainably produced fuel. Even better, if the charcoal is from a local producer, the carbon dioxide emissions generated by transporting it from the producer to the store can be reduced by as much as 85 per cent compared with imported charcoal. As coppicing creates the right conditions for many plants that provide food for butterflies to flourish, you will be helping to conserve threatened species too. So look for charcoal bags that say "locally produced" or "home grown".

Barbecuing using an empty clay pot couldn't be easier. You'll need a pot about 33cm (13in) in diameter to feed up to three people, a larger one for more people.

- Stand the pot on a couple or bricks to allow air to circulate underneath the fire. Fill the pot half full with pebbles or crocks (broken clay pots), slightly more if it is tall.
- Line the top part with kitchen foil and heap the charcoal in the centre. Use a proprietary barbecue lighter to light the coals.
- When the coals are glowing red and have started to turn grey at the edges, spread them out evenly and balance an oven shelf or grill pan shelf over the rim of the pot.
- Cook skewers of peppers, courgettes and mushrooms, or pieces of fish or meat, and throw a handful of rosemary, thyme or lavender on the fire for a hint of herby flavour as the skewers are cooking.

PLANT A TREE OR CLIMBER FOR WILDLIFE

Gardens, no matter how small, have become incredibly important havens for wildlife. This is because wild creatures have lost many of their feeding and breeding sites in the countryside – either as a result of intensive farming, which makes widespread use of pesticides, or changes in land use. Some creatures, such as moths, bumblebees and hedgehogs, are increasingly reliant on our gardens for their survival.

If all you have in your garden are a few containers with a selection of flowering plants, you will still have some wildlife: small soil creatures, visiting butterflies and hoverflies, perhaps, and, if you leave the seedheads on your plants, some seed-eating birds. You'll attract more creatures if your patch has some water, a shrub or two and a thick climber. But you can offer first-class living quarters to a host of wildlife if you have a small tree.

A tree can provide

- Plenty of leaves and nectar-rich flowers for insects and their larvae to feed on.
- Bark for insects to live in and for lichens and mosses with their attendant creatures.
- Berries and seeds for birds.
- A layer of leaves at the base of the tree that, if left to decay, creates food and shelter for worms, slugs, snails, woodlice and millipedes, which in turn provides food for centipedes, spiders and beetles.
- Dead and decaying wood, which provides food and nesting sites for creatures such as beetles or solitary bees. Eventually, holes in the trunk can create nesting sites for birds.

In a small garden, a tree will probably become the dominant feature, and if you choose a deciduous tree it will help to bring seasonal changes: new buds, followed by blossom in spring; a lush green canopy of leaves in summer; tawny, orange or red foliage, plus berries or seeds, in autumn; and a striking silhouette of branches to admire in winter.

Helping wildlife

● If you have only a roof terrace or balcony and no room for trees or climbers, grow a mixture of flowering plants (with single flowers rather than double) to provide a source of nectar for insects such as butterflies, moths and bees. You could also fill a shallow dish with water to make a bird bath, attach a lightweight bird feeder to a window or fix a nesting box to a wall at least two metres off the ground – numbers of sparrows have dropped dramatically in some areas in the UK and providing nest boxes may help to halt their decline.

● Researchers have found that, as far as insects and invertebrates are concerned, small gardens are just as good for wildlife as larger ones. In a survey of biodiversity in 61 private gardens ranging in size from 32–940sq m (344–10,000sq ft) in the city of Sheffield in the UK, the researchers caught and counted an astonishing 40,000 individual invertebrates, and found nationally rare beetles, bugs, snails and flies, and a spider that had only previously been recorded on a mountain top.

● Gardens make a vital network of wildlife habitats in major cities. In London, for example, 20 per-cent of all open space is occupied by private gardens.

Choose your wildlife plant

■ **Crab apples** *(Malus* spp*)* are ideal for small gardens, especially 'John Downie' (8 x 8m/25 x 25ft) or the weeping M x *scheideckeri* 'Red Jade' (4 x 4m/12 x 12ft). Insects will gorge on the blossom and birds love to devour the red or orange fruits.

■ **Hawthorns** *(Crataegus monogyna)* (8 x 8m/25 x 25ft) are magnets for caterpillars, which in turn provide food for countless birds. Hawthorns are tough, thorny trees with beautiful white blossom and bright red berries.

■ **Rowan trees** *(Sorbus* spp*)* also support lots of wildlife. The variety 'Joseph Rock' (8 x 8m/25 x 25ft) has white flowers and creamy-orange fruits.

■ If you don't have space for a tree, but can plant a climber, think about planting an ivy along a fence or wall. **Ivies** *(Hedera* spp*)* make wonderful curtains of greenery, can be grown on north-facing surfaces and are top-notch wildlife plants: they are associated with some 230 species of animal, from insects to nesting birds. Ivies are especially valuable as a late source of nectar for butterflies, and the winter berries attract birds. Ivies can be allowed to bush out for an informal look, or clipped to suit a more formally designed plot. If clipping ivy, make sure you wait until after the nesting season, as a secretive wren may have nested there. With a bushy ivy, a hedgehog may even take up residence behind the leafy apron at the base.

■ **Firethorns** *(Pyracantha* spp*)* also make excellent evergreen coverings for walls or fences, and their bounty of beautiful yellow, scarlet or orange berries will feed birds through the cold winter months.

PLANT VEGETABLES IN A "SQUARE FOOT" GARDEN

Even on a patio or balcony, you can grow your own mini vegetable garden with a selection of delicious vegetables – from lettuces to spring onions, radishes to dwarf beans. A square foot garden in a sunny patch is easier to manage than a series of pots, makes maximum use of space, and saves on seeds and time spent thinning or weeding – in fact, it's ideal for a novice gardener or for children.

A square foot garden is a raised bed that can be made on top of an area of existing soil, in which case it can be filled with the soil and enriched with garden compost and well-rotted manure. But it can also sit on top of a hard surface, such as paving, which is the method described here. If you can't fit in one 122cm by 122cm (4ft by 4ft) square, which produces 16 separate "plots", you could make one half this size, which would still give you four squares to grow four different vegetables.

Keep it organic

● Use untreated timber for the box.

● Fill with a mixture of topsoil (from building suppliers or bagged from garden centres), organic compost and a soil conditioner such as home-made leafmould or garden compost.

● To prevent a build-up of pests and diseases, practise crop rotation: avoid growing vegetables from the same family in the same square for more than one year in three or four.

● Courgettes, sweetcorn, Swiss chard, spinach and most salads can be grown before or after most other vegetables without problems and so are very useful in a square foot vegetable garden.

How it works

A square foot garden is contained inside a box or frame made of timber or, if bought ready-made, usually of recycled plastic. A grid dividing the box into 30cm (1ft) squares is then laid on top of the soil. This enables you to keep the squares separate so that you can manage the different crops. By keeping the box size 1.2m by 1.2m (4ft by 4ft), you will be able to reach all the squares without stepping on the soil, which can cause compaction. By using a weed-free nutrient-rich soil mix and planting vegetables closely together, you'll get high yields from your plants and something to pick or snip off right through the season.

■ **Construct a box** using four planks of wood 3cm (1¼in) thick and 20–25cm (8–10in) high. You need two planks 122cm (4ft) long and two planks 116cm (3ft 10in) long Take one 116cm (3ft 10in) length and onto each end screw one of the 122cm (4ft) lengths. Then attach the final 116cm (3ft 10in) length.

■ **Place in a sunny spot**, clear of trees and shade, where it will not puddle after heavy rain.

■ **Fill with soil** (*see* Keep it organic *box*) and make a grid to divide the garden into 30cm (1ft) squares, either by nailing lengths of cord or string across the area, or with pieces of wood screwed together and laid on top of the soil.

■ **Choose the types of vegetables** you want to eat – you don't have to stick to one square for each type of vegetable: peas, for example, which crop for a longer time if they have

Good vegetables to grow

❶ Spinach

❷ Chard

❸ Carrots

❹ French beans

❺ Lettuce

more space, would be better grown across two or three squares. Plan to have something to pick right through the summer and into autumn. Cut-and-come-again lettuces and herbs will provide you with leaves for many weeks, while herbs such as parsley and sweet marjoram can be picked all summer. Avoid slow-growing or deep-rooted crops such as cauliflower or sprouting broccoli. Site taller vegetables, such as beans or peas, at the back where they won't shade out the other plants

■ **Make a shallow planting hole**, drop in one or two seeds and cover with soil. Water in and leave to germinate. If more than one seedling appears, cut off the weaker one with a pair of scissors so as not to disturb the roots of the remaining plant.

■ **With bushy plants**, such as tomatoes, grow just one plant per square. With more compact plants such as lettuces, or dwarf varieties such as French bean 'Golden Sands' or sweetcorn 'Minipop', you can fit four per square. With baby vegetables such as the short-rooted carrot 'Amini' or early 'Nantes' cultivars, which are quick to mature, and with slim plants such as spring onions or radishes, you can grow up to 16 in one square.

■ **When you have harvested** a fast-maturing crop such as lettuce, you can plant a second crop of a later vegetable like Swiss chard in the same square, adding some fresh compost before you sow or plant out. When the crops have all been picked, refresh the soil by digging in well-rotted garden compost or manure, before sowing the following spring.

COLLECT & USE WATER EFFICIENTLY

In developed countries, we each use three times the amount of water considered sufficient by development agencies for a person's safe and hygienic cooking, washing and sanitation needs. With climate changes bringing hotter and drier summers, more development on wetland sites and increased housing needs, water stores – which rely on underground and reservoir water – will soon be severely depleted.

At the moment, the water we use outside only accounts for about six per cent of our domestic water use, but the demand for water in our homes is a third higher in summer than in winter – largely because we are watering our plants. In fact, up to 70 per cent of the water demand on a summer's evening is due to garden use. And it's expected that the amount we pour onto our gardens will continue to increase. For these reasons, we should try to use less water in the garden, and to water in the most efficient way we can.

One of the best things anyone with outdoor space can do is to store rainwater so that you can use it to water plants and top up water features or bird baths, especially in periods of no rain. Water butts are widely available in various sizes, shapes and materials (usually recycled plastic or wood), and many local authorities offer them at discounted prices to encourage gardeners to use them. A butt can be connected to a down pipe with a simple diverter kit, which also prevents the butt from overflowing. If you have space, you can even connect a second butt to the first one, and install others to catch rain from sheds or flat roofs.

How to use a water butt

■ Stand each butt on a strong platform – special stands are available – so that you can fit a watering can easily under the tap at the bottom.

■ Put a lid on the butt to make it childproof, and to keep the water clean and minimize evaporation.

■ Water your plants at the coolest times of the day and direct the water at the roots.

Water your plants efficiently

■ Add organic matter, such as garden compost or organic soil conditioner, to the soil to improve its structure.

■ Put a layer of mulch, such as bark chips or gravel, around the plants to slow down evaporation from the soil and to suppress weeds.

■ Grow plants that are suited to the conditions in your garden. If it gets very dry and hot in the summer, choose plenty of drought-tolerant plants, which often have silvery leaves and are sometimes downy or waxy.

■ Use water-retaining granules or gel in pots and line them with perforated plastic.

■ If using containers, choose large ones.

■ For very thirsty plants in containers, push a watering spike into the soil, which releases drops into the soil as and when the plants need moisture.

■ Pour water from a can directly over the root area of each plant in the coolest parts of the day so that most of it does not evaporate.

■ Don't use sprinklers: if automatic irrigation systems, such as drip or seep pipes that allow water to drip into the soil, are permitted by your water authority, use these instead, especially for times when you are away from the garden.

■ In periods of drought, make use of grey water such as bath or shower water, which can be channelled from a downpipe into the garden (make sure that you only use natural bath products in the bath or shower). You can also use washing-up water, as long as it contains no chemicals (eco-detergent is fine, as it won't harm plants). Don't store this water for more than 24 hours, and don't use it on plants you intend to eat. You can also make a small depression around each plant to contain as much moisture as possible after watering or rain falls.

Did you know?

● If you leave a sprinkler on for an hour, it can use the same amount of water that a family of four normally uses in two days.

● Watering during the hottest part of the day can mean that 90% of the water evaporates.

GROW POTS OF TOMATOES

The most delicious summer tomatoes are those that you can pick, sun-ripened, straight from a plant that's growing outdoors – the flavour and aroma are more intense than shop-bought ones, or even those raised in greenhouses.

Growing your own tomatoes saves you money – half a dozen plants with good yields should keep a family of four stocked with succulent fruits right through the summer season – and it allows you to grow a range of different and unusual varieties. Choose from cherry-sized salad tomatoes, plums (ideal for sauces), large fleshy varieties such as "Marmande" and even yellow, orange, or striped tomato fruits. Outdoor tomatoes generally have fewer pests and diseases than greenhouse ones and so are easier to manage. In a tiny garden, you can grow them very successfully in pots – the larger the container, the better – or in growbags against a sunny wall.

Tomatoes grow either as cordons – tall, single-stemmed plants known as indeterminates, trained to a support and with side shoots and the main growing point nipped out to speed up ripening – or as bush types. Bush tomatoes grow from 30 to 75cm (12–30in) tall and sprawl out. They don't yield as big a crop as cordons, but they are easy to grow and don't need supports or pinching out. Dwarf varieties of bush types are often no more than 20cm (8in) high, and because they trail they are ideal for windowboxes or hanging baskets.

How to grow tomatoes

Tomatoes are tender plants, so they shouldn't be put outdoors while there's a risk of frost. They need a sunny, sheltered spot to ripen, and when grown in containers or growbags they need to be regularly watered and fed.

Grow tomatoes from seed

■ Tomato seeds need a minimum temperature of 16°C (61°F) to germinate.

■ Sow them 6–8 weeks before a last frost is due, either in a seed tray or 2–3 seeds to a 9cm (3½in) pot or module.

■ Once 2–3 leaves have appeared, transplant the seedlings into individual pots in a light, well-ventilated spot.

■ Harden the seedlings off by leaving them outside for several hours during the day before planting out.

Or buy young tomato plants

■ Buy the plants from a grower or your local garden centre.

■ Plant in loam-based compost when the first cluster of flowers (trusses) are visible. Cordon types, which can be planted in growbags, need canes or sticks at least 1.5m (5ft) tall to support them.

■ As the plants grow, tie the main stems to the supports. Remove any side shoots in mid- to late summer, usually when four trusses have formed, and nip off the main growing point.

Growing tips

● If you are using growbags, make sure that they contain peat-free compost.

● Ensure that your container or pot has drainage holes.

● Tomatoes in pots and growbags need regular feeding. Use an organic feed that is rich in potash.

● Water regularly and don't let the plants dry out: a handful of water-storage gel or granules in the compost will help to retain moisture. A growbag positioned in direct sunlight can require more than two watering cans full of water a day.

● Don't let the plants become waterlogged: this causes the skins of the fruit to split.

● Grow marigolds with the plants to help deter whitefly.

● Pick the fruits as they ripen by snapping them off at the swelling on the stalk, using a thumb and finger. Before the first frosts, take off any unripened tomatoes and store them in a dark, dry place, such as a drawer or in a box in a cupboard, with an apple or banana. These fruits will give off ethylene, a chemical that accelerates ripening.

Choose your tomato plant

Try one, or even two if you have the space, of these varieties, which all grow well in pots or growbags in a sunny, sheltered site. Other good varieties include Marmande for large fruits and Sungold, which has orange cherry fruits with an excellent flavour.

❶ Garden Pearl Heavy crops of pinkish cherry tomatoes; trailer.

❷ Gold Nugget Yellow fruits; bush.

❸ Gardener's Delight A heavy cropper with deliciously sweet, deep red cherry fruits; cordon.

❹ Nectar Very tasty cherry tomatoes; cordon.

❺ Tumbler Masses of sweet red fruits; trailer.

❻ Roma VF Heavy cropping plum; bush.

❼ Tiny Tim Tasty cherry fruits; trailer.

❽ Big Boy Giant fruits; cordon.

❾ Red alert Small, oval fruits; early variety of bush.

Did you know?

Tomatoes grown in Europe in the 1520s were used as ornamentals since the fruit was thought to be poisonous – the foliage is, in fact, poisonous.

Tomato salad with goat's cheese & basil dressing

(serves four)

If you have a good yield of tomatoes and grow your own salad leaves, try this recipe to bring out the best in your home-grown ingredients.

Ingredients

350g (1½lb) vine-ripened tomatoes

4 handfuls mixed salad leaves (rocket, mizuna, frisée, chicory, cress)

1 tablespoon balsamic vinegar

150ml (5fl oz) olive oil

A handful of fresh basil

A pinch of salt and black pepper

85g (3oz) mild, creamy goat's cheese

Method

■ Cut the tomatoes into chunks and put into a bowl.

■ Place the salad leaves in another bowl.

■ Blend the vinegar, olive oil, basil and seasoning together to make a thick dressing. Pour half over the tomatoes and carefully mix. Pour the other half over the salad leaves and gently mix.

■ Divide the salad leaves between four plates, top with a serving each of the tomatoes, crumble some of the cheese over each portion and serve.

GARDEN WITHOUT PESTICIDES

With the possibility that many common garden pesticides have hormone-displacing properties and links to cancer, or can poison pets and hedgehogs if eaten in large quantities, the safest option is not to use pesticides at all. There are plenty of natural ways to deal with pests, diseases or unwanted plants or weeds.

To keep pests to a minimum, the first thing you should do is grow your plants well. That means growing them in well-drained, organically fed soil in the right conditions and with the right amount of moisture for each plant. Keeping beds and containers weed-free will give plants the best growing conditions.

Encourage natural predators

There are a whole raft of natural predators at your disposal, from insects, beetles and birds to frogs, toads, hedgehogs, bats, slowworms and shrews. In order to establish a natural balance in your garden, you will have to tolerate a low level of pests so that the predators have enough to feed on. You also need to think about providing your allies with shelter, other food and water. Insects generally like to shelter in undisturbed, dark places such as log piles, under stones or a mound of ground-cover plants or in the hollow stems of plants. They also need a supply of nectar and pollen, which you can provide with a selection of plants. Birds need nesting sites – natural places like thick curtains of ivy or honeysuckle, dense

Tips for natural solutions

● Be prepared to put up with the odd nibbled leaf. An insect such as the leaf cutter bee cuts neat semicircles out of rose leaves for its nest, but it is also a useful pollinator.

● Use your fingers and thumbs to pick off large pests such as caterpillars, lily beetles or snails (easy to spot at night, with a torch) and to knock off aphids from stems and leaves.

● Plant-based insecticides, which break down quickly and don't stay in the environment, are available for organic gardeners but remember they will kill off other insects, including beneficial ones, as well as the ones you are targeting.

● The best way to avoid diseases is to grow strong, healthy plants in organically managed soil.

● Grow as many different flowering plants with a mixture of flower types as you can and try to make sure there's something in flower right through the season. That way, there'll be nectar and pollen for a wide variety of beneficial insects.

shrubs and trees, or artificial ones – and, depending on the species of bird, food such as seeds, nuts and berries. Frogs and toads require damp places, while hedgehogs need somewhere dry and undisturbed.

You can also introduce parasitic worms, called nematodes, which occur naturally and target specific pests such as vine weevils, slugs, caterpillars and leatherjackets. They can be bought in powdered form and usually watered in once the soil reaches a minimum temperature of 5°C (41°F). You may need to apply them twice in a season. Set up barriers to prevent pests reaching seedlings and vulnerable plants (certain plants are beacons for some pests – for example, hostas and dahlias for slugs and snails). Copper tape around pots, or copper mats underneath them, and sharp, dry barriers around plants in the ground can help keep slugs and snails away. Or you can drown them in shallow bowls of beer or fruit juice, set just above the surface of the soil so that beetles don't fall in. Collect earwigs, which can polish off young seedlings, in upturned flowerpots filled with straw, and then dispose of them. Horticultural fleece fixed over carrots will keep root flies away, as will matting around cabbages.

Organic allies in the garden

■ **Ladybirds** Adults and larvae eat aphids.

■ **Hoverflies** Larvae eat aphids.

■ **Social wasps** Eat aphids, caterpillars and flies.

■ **Ichneumon wasps** Larvae eat caterpillars, some adults eat aphids.

■ **Ground beetles** Eat slugs, snails and other soil-living creatures.

■ **Spiders** Eat aphids and flying pests.

■ **Lacewings** Larvae eat aphids.

■ **Tachinid flies** Eat caterpillars and other grubs.

■ **Devil's coach-horse beetles** Feed on different types of invertebrate.

■ **Birds** Blue and great tits, robins, wrens, house sparrows and blackbirds depend on huge quantities of grubs for their chicks. Adult birds such as house sparrows, tits and chaffinches feed on aphids and other insects. Blackbirds and thrushes eat slugs and snails.

■ **Frogs, toads, newts & hedgehogs** Eat slugs.

GROW SWEET PEAS FOR CUTTING

One of the most wonderful sights and scents of summer is a vase of freshly picked sweet peas (*Lathyrus odoratus*) in shades of pink, white, yellow, blue, purple and burgundy. By growing your own you can pick a bunch every couple of days – and the more you pick, the longer your plants will produce flowers through the summer months.

Sweet peas are climbers, so they need some wires or netting to scramble up a fence or wall, or a tall, free-standing support. In a small outdoor space you can use a wigwam or obelisk in a bed or large pot. The wigwam will quickly be covered in the flowers, making a delightful, richly scented feature. Old-fashioned sweet peas have a stronger, spicier fragrance than modern varieties (if you buy modern sweet peas, lavenders, blues and pale colours are often the most fragrant).

Sweet peas need

- A sunny, open spot.

- Soil that's had manure or organic compost added to it before planting.

- A good mulch of manure or compost after planting.

- Tying onto the support for the first few weeks of growth.

- Regular watering, especially in dry, sunny weather.

- Picking every couple of days once the flowers appear; once the plants seed they won't produce more flowers.

Make a wigwam

You can buy ready-made obelisks, but it's much more fun – and cheaper – to make your own using bamboo canes or, for a rustic-style wigwam, hazel or willow rods. Annual sweet peas will grow to 1.8m (6ft) or more in a season, so the poles need to be 1.8–2m (6ft) long. Prepare the soil first *(see left)*, then space out six poles to form a circle, pushing them into the ground or the base of a pot and securing them at the top with string or a purpose-made disc, available from garden centres. For extra support, you can weave in some clippings from any flexible-stemmed plants you may have growing, such as clematis, Virginia creeper or dogwood, or tie in lengths of string or raffia.

How to grow sweet peas

You can buy sweet peas as young plants from garden centres and plant fairs but, if you have time, you can grow your own from seed. Make sure that you choose one of the richly scented varieties – some sweet peas are bred for the shape and size of their flowers – and either sow the seeds under cover in a cold frame or greenhouse in late winter, or outdoors at the foot of the wigwam rods in early- and mid-spring.

If growing from seed, there's no need to chip the seed coat (which was the traditional method of preparing them) as long as you soak the potting compost well before burying the seeds in it.

■ Plant just one seed in an 8cm (3in) pot, or 6–8 seeds in a 15cm (6in) pot or in root trainers. Cover with newspaper until the seedlings appear.

■ When the first four leaves have formed, take off the top two leaves to encourage the plant to bush out. Harden the seedlings off well before planting them out, and be prepared to cover them with fleece if there's a cold snap.

■ If you prefer to sow straight into the ground, space out the seeds 20–30cm (8–12in) apart.

■ Once the first seedlings appear, or when you have planted out the young plants, tie them onto the support and continue to tie new stems in weekly for the first couple of months. As soon as the first flowers appear, start picking them.

Good varieties of sweet pea

All these old-fashioned varieties will cover a wigwam, have masses of small flowers and are richly scented:

'Black Knight': deep maroon/violet flowers.
'Dorothy Eckford': white flowers.
'Flora Norton': clear blue flowers.
'Henry Eckford': bright orange flowers.
'Lord Nelson': rich, dark blue flowers.
'Matacuna': rich maroon and purple flowers; one of the oldest varieties.
'Mrs Collier': rich cream-coloured flowers.
'Painted Lady': bicoloured pink flowers; the oldest variety of sweet pea in existence.

GROW HERBS FOR TEAS & INFUSIONS

Make your own herb teas and infusions from plants growing outside your kitchen window and get the very best flavour, aroma and healing properties from the freshly picked leaves.

For centuries, herbs have been used to make relaxing or refreshing drinks, and for infusions to help relieve a whole range of ailments from headaches to sore throats and indigestion. You can buy many of these herbs dried, in sachets, from supermarkets and health stores, but the drinks taste much better if you use fresh leaves. Fresh herbs are less concentrated than dried ones, so you'll need to use more (usually twice as much). If you grow them yourself, you'll have plenty of leaves, flowers and seeds to brew yourself a healthy, non-caffeinated drink – served hot in winter, cool in summer – whenever you feel like it. Many of these herbs have very pretty leaves and flowers too, so they make excellent plants for windowboxes or containers.

Medicinal benefits

Some herbs make pleasant tasting drinks that also have medicinal properties: peppermint, for example, aids digestion. Other herb infusions are mainly taken as natural remedies, such as sage, which has antiseptic properties and can be used as a gargle and mouth rinse. Sage tea can be sweetened with honey and drunk as a remedy for a cold, but can be toxic if over-used.

How to make a herb tea or infusion

Most herb teas have a light, delicate flavour so two or three teaspoons of fresh leaves are usually enough for a cup of herb tea, although just a single sprig of fresh rosemary in a cup makes a refreshing pick-me-up. Chamomile tea is made from the flowers, which should only be steeped for 3–4 minutes.

● Use freshly picked leaves. Crush the leaves on a piece of kitchen paper to release the oils.

● Put the leaves in a cup or tea pot and pour on just-boiled water. Cover tightly and leave to steep for 5–15 minutes, depending on the thickness of the leaves.

Growing tips

- Make sure that the plant pot has at least one drainage hole and a layer of broken clay pieces or gravel at the bottom of the pot.

- Most herbs need a minimum depth of 20cm (8in) to grow, but tall plants such as fennel need at least 30cm (12in) depth.

- Invasive herbs such as peppermint and lemon balm are best grown alone, as are large plants such as rosemary. Herbs such as sage, thyme and hyssop can be grouped together and grown in one pot.

- Most herbs need well-drained soil, and will collapse if they are waterlogged.

Choose your herbs

Most herbs prefer a sunny position, but many are robust plants and will cope with partial shade too, so give them a go. Protect the plants from extreme cold and don't let them become waterlogged.

1 **Lavender (*Lavandula*)**
Pick the flowers just as they open. Use an infusion of flowers for insomnia, loss of appetite and poor circulation.

2 **Fennel (*Foeniculum vulgare*)**
Harvest the seeds as they turn brown, and dry them well. Then crush them and add just boiled water. Use to remedy flatulence, indigestion, coughs and bronchitis.

3 **Rosemary (*Rosmarinus officinalis*)**
Pick leaves all year. Use as a gargle for a sore mouth and bad breath. Drink as a tea in small amounts to reduce flatulence. As an infusion, it conditions hair and makes it shine.

4 **Chamomile (*Chamaemelum nobile*)**
Pick the flowers just as the petals curl back. Use as a calming drink for indigestion and insomnia. Can be used as a gargle or mouthwash.

5 **Hyssop (*Hyssopus officinalis*)**
Pick young leaves through the growing season. Use an infusion of leaves for coughs and respiratory congestion. Avoid during pregnancy.

6 **Lemon balm (*Melissa officinalis*)**
Pick the leaves before the flowers open. Use for headaches and tension, indigestion and flatulence.

7 **Peppermint (*Mentha spicata*)**
Perennial that can be fed with comfrey to give a new crop of tender leaves each year. Use for indigestion, nausea, flatulence, colds and, served cold, to bring down fevers.

8 **Sage (*Salvia officinalis*)**
Choose the grey-green non-variegated common sage for the most intense flavour and most potent medicinal properties. Pick leaves throughout the year; they have a milder flavour before flowering. Use as a gargle for sore throats and mouth sores. Can also be drunk to soothe indigestion, but should not be taken during pregnancy.

9 **Thyme (*Thymus*)**
Pick leaves all year round. Use as a gargle for sore throats, sore gums and a sore mouth. Also said to be good for hangovers.

MAKE YOUR OWN COMPOST

Even if you only have a small outside space, it's worth thinking about making your own compost. Not only will it take your organic kitchen, household and garden waste – much of which would otherwise go straight to landfill sites – it also presents you with your own free supply of compost, which you can use to feed and condition the soil and add to potting mixes for plants in containers. If your space is too tiny to fit a compost bin, check to see if you can send your organic waste to a centralized composting scheme, such as those run by local authorities or community groups.

The easiest, neatest way to make compost in a small space is in a ready-made compost bin. Most are made from recycled plastic, but if the bin has to be positioned in view there are also attractive wooden beehive-shaped bins, which can be painted or stained any colour you want. Most come without a base so that they can stand on top of the soil – this allows the micro-organisms in the soil and larger composting worms and beetles to move up through the material in the bin, composting as they go. If you do not have access to soil, choose a bin with a base and start off with a layer of soil, adding some more if you can as your heap builds up.

There are two ways of making compost: if you have a lot of material to start with, you can go the "hot route": filling the bin with well-mixed, moistened brown and green matter *(see box, right)* and turning the heap, which will quickly heat up, several times over a few weeks to speed up the aerobic work of the microbes. You can have dark brown, earthy smelling compost in six to eight weeks. For most people with small gardens, and those with less time on their hands, the "cool route" works best (*see below*). Place the bin in a warm, sheltered spot.

Cool composting

■ Put a few woody plant stems at the bottom of the bin to help improve air circulation and drainage.

■ Add a good layer of mixed green and brown items *(right)*. Always chop tougher, bigger stems into small pieces. Unless they are already wet, water them with a watering can.

■ Carry on filling the bin. Don't put in too much sloppy green waste in one go – mix it up with bulkier items.

■ Water the heap if it looks dry.

■ If the heap looks soggy, turn it with a fork and add some more bulky material.

■ The material will eventually rot down. After a few months, check the bottom part. If it looks dark brown and well rotted, dig it out and use in the garden. Mix up the rest, water it if it seems dry and leave in the bin to carry on composting.

The right bin

■ Holds at least 200 litres (53 gallons); the more well-mixed material it contains, the greater the biological activity.

■ Has a lid, to keep rain out and heat in.

■ Has a good-sized opening at the top to fork in garden waste, and is either easy to lift off to get at the compost when it's ready or has an access door or panel at the bottom.

What to put in

All compost heaps need a good mix of "greens" – soft green matter that is high in nitrogen – and "browns" – tougher plants that take longer to rot and are high in carbon. If you put in a lot of kitchen waste, add bulkier items such as cardboard and egg boxes.

Must have

Greens and browns
Annual non-flowering weeds
Grass cuttings
Fruit and vegetable scraps
Woody clippings and prunings
Leaves of non-coniferous trees and shrubs: eg, ash, elm, lime, poplar, willow, sycamore, elder
Sawdust and wood shavings

Also good

Tea bags, coffee grounds, egg shells and wood ash
Egg boxes, cereal boxes and other bits of cardboard
Crumpled or shredded paper towels and newspaper
Wool
Old straw and hay, gerbil, hamster and rabbit bedding

Leave out

Meat, fish and cooked food
Weed seeds
Diseased plant material
Disposable nappies, dog or cat faeces
Glossy newsprint
Coal ash

GROW CHILLI PEPPERS IN A POT

Even if you only grow them for the look of their bright, shiny fruits, chilli plants can add an exotic element to your patio or balcony in summer. Chillies grow as perennials in their native South America, but they can also be raised as annuals indoors when grown from seed. This means that you can experiment with different varieties – and different degrees of fieriness – to flavour sauces, marinades and spicy dishes, just for the price of a packet of seeds and some compost.

Specialist growers raise chillies in greenhouses or polytunnels, which provide the plants with the warmth they need for germination and the light for the seedling stage. But you can also start them off on a bright windowsill, as long as the temperature is 21°C (70°F). The easiest way to ensure this is by using a heated mat or propagator. Use a free-draining compost, and water well before sowing in small pots. Space a few seeds evenly on the surface of each pot and cover with perlite. As soon as the seedlings emerge and are showing two leaves, transfer to small pots (7.5cm/3in in diameter) and move them to a spot where they will get plenty of daylight. Keep them warm, moist and well ventilated. When the plants have five pairs of leaves, transfer into bigger pots. Once there is no danger of frost, harden off the plants by leaving the pots outdoors in a sheltered spot for up to ten days, bringing them in at night. Then leave them outdoors once the night-time temperature has reached 15°C (59°F).

Chillies in pots need
- Well-drained soil.
- Minimum night-time temperature of 15°C (59°F).
- Liquid feed every 1–2 weeks once flowers appear.
- Regular picking to encourage more fruit to form.

Hot tips

- The more mature the chilli, the hotter it is.

- The white pith, with the seeds attached, is the hottest part.

- The fieriness is caused by the alkaloid (chemical compound) capsaicin, and the amount each pepper contains varies depending on the variety, soil, climate and even its position on the plant.

- A chilli's heat is measured in Scoville Units. Mild chillies contain about 600 units, while the habaneros types range from 200,000–350,000 units.

- Always avoid touching your eyes or other tender areas after handling chillies. If you have sensitive skin, wear gloves when preparing any chillies.

- If you've eaten too hot a chilli, have milk or yoghurt.

Good varieties to grow

Filius blue Fruits mature from green to purple to red; medium to hot.

Aurora Fruits mature from green to purple to orange red; very hot.

Cherry bomb Cherry-shaped red fruits; medium hot.

Twilight Green, red and purple fruits; very hot.

USE RECLAIMED WOOD & FURNITURE

Nowadays, our wood and furniture can be sourced from all over the world. Softwoods such as pine may come from the forests of northern Europe or Russia; tropical hardwoods like teak and mahogany from Africa, Brazil or Asia. Unfortunately, much of the global timber industry is currently unsustainable. Virgin forests are being clear-felled, and plantations are much less valuable for wildlife than the forests they are replacing. Using wood carefully, without waste, is a way of treating this natural product with the respect it deserves.

A new lease of life

The best environmental choice is to repair, restore or adapt furniture rather than replace it. You may need professional help, but it could still be cheaper than buying new and is far better for the world's forests.

■ Be creative with your existing furniture. An old sofa can be re-covered or livened up with a bright throw. Battered wooden furniture can be stripped and re-painted, waxed, stained or stencilled.

■ Re-doing your floor? Check if your existing wooden floorboards can be sanded and used again.

■ If you are discarding furniture, consider selling it or donating to a furniture exchange charity.

■ Buy in antique and secondhand shops.

■ Consider commissioning furniture from professional designers. They can source reclaimed wood and you will get a unique piece of artwork.

Second-hand and reclaimed timber

■ Old wood has a unique beauty. Nowadays, timber trees rarely grow for more than 30 or 40 years.

■ Old timber is more likely to be from a tree that lived for over a century, developing a beautiful dense grain and colour.

■ Reclaimed wood is often much cheaper than virgin wood.

Where to find reclaimed wood and reusable furniture

Salvage companies and reclaimed timber merchants. Reclaimed wood can be sourced from remodelled or demolished buildings, disused railway sleepers or even the legs from an old table.

Adverts in local papers.

Skips (get permission first).

Your local authority may have information on timber recycling and furniture exchange schemes.

The facts on wood

● Natural forests are being destroyed to make way for faster-growing "factory forests" for timber and paper production, threatening the survival of many species of trees, plants and animals. Each year, about 13 million hectares of the world's forests are lost to deforestation.

● Deforestation accounts for up to 20% of global CO_2 emissions: vast amounts of carbon are released into the atmosphere when natural forests are destroyed.

● The UN predicts a 58% increase in wood consumption over the next 20 years.

3 GARDEN, ALLOTMENT OR FIELD

KEEP SOME CHICKENS

If you're thinking of keeping livestock for the first time, chickens are a good place to start. They will provide you with a continuing supply of tasty and nutritious eggs, and can be pleasant company.

Chickens are entertaining characters to have around your garden, and are an ideal, low-maintenance introduction to keeping your own birds and animals. Depending on the breed, you can expect to have around 200 eggs or more per year, or tasty, organically reared meat when you want it. Chickens are also the perfect partners in an organic lifestyle. If you grow your own food, you can use a movable chicken run or "ark" to help prepare the ground for sowing. The hens will scratch at the surface of the soil, breaking it up, eat pests and weeds and apply their own organic fertilizer, which is rich in nitrogen. In return, they are comparatively easy to look after, requiring only a little care, grain to eat, somewhere to roam and housing where they can lay their eggs and roost at night.

Buying your birds

Chickens are available either as hybrids, which have generally been bred to lay larger numbers of eggs, or as pure breeds – the traditional breeds – which are hardier and more disease-resistant, tend to lay eggs from March to September, and can be used for meat. If you buy chicks, you won't be able to tell their sex, which means that you may end up with more than one male bird – you only need a cockerel if you want to breed chickens, which is worthwhile if you keep pure breeds. Young hens ready to produce eggs are called pullets, and are usually "at point of lay" at 18–20 weeks old. Look through poultry and smallholder magazines or contact private breeders for young hens for sale. Ask to see the parent stock before you buy.

It's best to buy just two or three young egg-laying hens to start with. Hens are most productive when they are young, providing a supply of eggs for between two to five years. They lay fewer eggs as they age, so it's worth thinking about slowly introducing a few more hens over time to build a flock that can provide you with a constant supply of eggs.

When new birds arrive, shut them in their own house overnight with some food and water. Gently open the low exit hatch the next morning and, if they find their way out without pressure, they will return to their house again in the evening.

The best way to handle poultry

Handle your hens regularly to check that they are well and haven't lost weight. You can, with practice, use a fishing landing net to catch a hen, then place both hands around her wings and body and lift her, without squeezing, to face you, talking and moving slowly all the time. Slide one hand under her, rest her weight on your forearm, hold her close to your body and inspect her. Pick up all poultry this way (never hold them upside-down by one leg).

Signs of good health in a chicken

- Dry nostrils.
- Bright eyes.
- A red comb (some breeds have naturally dark combs).
- Shiny feathers (all present).
- Good weight and musculature for age.
- Clean vent (rear-end) feathers with no smell.
- Smooth shanks.
- Straight toes.
- Alert and active.

Stay aware of any news on avian flu, and take advice from Defra.

Top three most popular pure breeds

Welsummer

Cuckoo Marans

Lavender Araucana

Choose your chickens

Chickens can be bought in two sizes: as small birds, or bantams, and as full-size birds. The lightweight bantams are ideal for a small garden, but the larger birds are usually more docile and sociable. The chickens shown here are all pure breeds, well-suited to free-range life.

Lavender Araucana
Lays blue eggs. Called "Ameraucana" in the US.

Barred Plymouth Rock
Very good layer of light brown eggs. Easy to keep.

Blue Laced Wyandotte
Large and bantam breeds. Fair layers. Eggs often small.

Appenzeller Spitzhauben
Very active; requires large runs and high fences.

Buff Sussex
Large and bantam breeds. Easy for beginners to keep.

Welsummer
Lays dark brown eggs. Great choice for gardens.

Partridge Rumpless Araucana
Lays blue or olive-green eggs. From South America.

Silver Laced Wyamdotte
Lays tinted eggs. Fair layers, but eggs often small.

Rhode Island Red
Lays brown eggs. Good choice for small flocks.

Cuckoo Marans
Lays dark brown eggs. Good table bird.

Gold Pencilled Hamburgh
Lays white eggs. Requires large runs and high fences.

Light Sussex
Large and bantam breeds. Good table bird.

Hybrid varieties

These hardy breeds are docile, reliable egg layers.

Mrs Pepperpot
Superb layer of large to extra-large brown eggs. Easy to handle.

Black Rock
Steady layer and disease-resistant. Docile, but full of character.

Speckledy Hen
Easy to handle. Prolific egg layer of dark, chestnut-brown eggs.

Looking after your chickens

Watch your birds every day for signs of ill-health, for example, hens that keep their heads down, eyes closed or refuse to eat, drink or lay. Check their feed and contact a vet if signs persist. Only treat birds for parasites, such as worms or lice, as they occur. If you are keeping chickens for their eggs, watch out for broody behaviour – birds that are reluctant to leave their nest box or become angry when they are disturbed. Remove any eggs and shut them out of their nest box for a few days.

Your hens will moult every autumn, becoming quite scraggy – even virtually featherless – from November until February. This is quite normal, and they won't lay during this period.

What you'll need

Hen house A ventilated hen house or coop provides nesting boxes for laying and a place to roost at night, safe from predators. Line the nest boxes with clean straw, and ensure they are in a dark area – hens like dark, secret places to lay their eggs. Clean out the house once a week. Use gloves and a scraper to clean off the droppings and disinfect the floor. Dust for lice every three weeks. If you have broody or new hens, it's a good idea to have another hen house, or section off one area, to separate them for a while.

Free roaming or a run You can allow your hens to wander freely around your garden every day, as they will find their way back to their roost at night. Keep their food and water in their house to deter wild birds. If the chickens are under threat from predators during the day, use a run to protect them, and move it to a new site every so often.

Feed & water Hens need a diet of fresh grain in addition to the insects and seeds they find in the garden. Grit is also essential and should always be available, as it helps them to break down and digest their food. They will also happily feed on green leftovers and cooked rice and pasta (but not meat or fish), from your kitchen. Clear any excess feed away every day to reduce the chances of attracting vermin. Always provide constant supplies of fresh water.

A chicken keeper's kit

❶ Automatic feeders
will keep food dry.

❷ Fresh water
Some water containers automatically top up as the chickens drink from them.

❸ Feed
Use an organic corn mix and protein pellets from reputable suppliers. Keep food fresh and sealed.

❹ Straw
Use clean straw, newspaper or shredded cardboard to line the house.

❺ Hen house
The house must be vermin-proof and provide 40sq cm (16sq in) of space for each hen. Don't use creosote to paint any bird or animal houses, as it is toxic. If you don't want to let your birds run free-range, their run should be as large as possible (ideally 8sq m/24sq ft for a few birds) and covered with strong wire netting to prevent them from escaping and predators from entering. Always keep your hen house clean.

MAKE SIMPLE CHUTNEYS & PICKLES

Autumn provides us with an abundant choice of foods to eat. Preserving some of the harvest means that nothing goes to waste, and extends the season into the winter months when there is less choice. The preserving process transforms flavours and textures, creating complex chutneys and pickles that will keep for weeks, months and sometimes even years. Salt, sugar, vinegar and alcohol can all be used to preserve the foods, which should be sealed in airtight, sterilized jars (wash the jars well and place in a moderate oven for five minutes to sterilize them).

Pickled turnips

Ingredients

1.4kg (3lb) turnips, peeled
700ml (1½ pints) white wine vinegar
110g (4oz) unrefined organic sugar
1 tablespoon salt
300ml (½ pint) olive oil

Method

■ Baby turnips can just be topped and tailed. Large turnips need cutting into neat shapes.
■ Put the vinegar, sugar and salt into a large stainless steel saucepan and slowly bring to the boil. Add the turnips and simmer for ten minutes.
■ Remove the pan from the heat and allow to cool.
■ Sterilize glass jars and fill with the vegetable

and vinegar mixture. When the jars are almost full, pour a thick layer of olive oil over the top.

■ Seal the jars and store them in a cupboard.

Variations

Pickled celeriac

Scrub and peel 1.4kg (3lb) celeriac and cut into wedges. Proceed as above, adding a few celery seeds and a good grinding of black pepper to the jars before covering with olive oil and sealing.

Pickled red peppers

Cut 1.4kg (3lb) red peppers in half, remove the seeds and cut each half into three. Proceed as above, adding sprigs of rosemary and a bay leaf to each jar before covering with olive oil.

Sauerkraut

Sauerkraut enhances intestinal health, promotes the growth of beneficial intestinal organisms and improves nutrient absorption. It's also high in antioxidants, especially vitamin C.

Ingredients

2 large white cabbage heads
2 tablespoons salt

Method

■ Finely shred the cabbage with a sharp knife or in a food processor.

■ Put the cabbage in a stainless steel bowl with 1 tablespoon of salt and pound well until some of the juices start to flow. The flat end of a wooden rolling pin is excellent for this job. Loosely cover with a cloth and leave for 24 hours.

■ Rinse out a 2 litre (3½ pint) glass jar. Put about 5cm (2in) of cabbage in the bottom of the jar, sprinkle with a little of the remaining salt and press down firmly. Continue until the cabbage is used up, leaving some space at the top of the jar (the cabbage will expand during fermentation).

■ Cover the mouth of the jar with parchment paper and place a weight on top. This weight forces water out of the cabbage, and then keeps the cabbage submerged under the brine until the sauerkraut is ready to be eaten. Some cabbage may not contain a lot of water. If the brine doesn't rise above the weight level after one day, add a little water to cover the cabbage.

■ Let the jar sit in a well-ventilated space at room temperature. After a week the cabbage will have fermented sufficiently to be eaten.

■ Cover the top with a plate and store in the fridge, where it will last for at least one month.

Variations

Caraway & coriander sauerkraut

Grind 1 tablespoon of mixed caraway and coriander seeds in a pestle and mortar or other grinder. Mix the seeds with the cabbage before layering in the jar.

Seaweed sauerkraut

Replace the salt with a handful of dried seaweed (approx 25g/1oz). Cut into small pieces, soak in warm water to rehydrate for 30 minutes, then drain well. Proceed as above, but fill the jar with alternate layers of cabbage and seaweed.

Pumpkin & apricot chutney

Ingredients

250g (9oz) red onions, chopped

A large chunk of fresh root ginger, grated

3 cloves of garlic, finely chopped

1 large chilli, finely chopped

2 tablespoons olive oil, plus a little for roasting

A large pinch each of cumin powder, coriander powder, salt and pepper

300g (10oz) dried apricots, whole

500ml (1 pint) cider vinegar

300g (10oz) unrefined organic sugar

200g (7oz) sultanas

250ml (½ pint) water

1 bay leaf

500g (1lb) pumpkin, peeled, deseeded and cubed

Method

■ In a thick-based pan, cook the onions, ginger, garlic and chilli in the olive oil until tender.

■ Add the rest of the ingredients, except the pumpkin, to the pan and bring to the boil. Simmer for one hour, stirring occasionally.

■ Meanwhile, toss the pumpkin cubes in a little olive oil and roast in a hot oven until they have taken on some colour and are soft.

■ Add the pumpkin to the chutney and simmer for a further 10 minutes. Remove from the heat.

■ Sterilize some glass jars and fill with the chutney. Fasten the lids securely and store in a cool, dry place for up to six months.

HEAT WATER NATURALLY

A quarter of the energy used in our homes is required to heat water. During the summer, and for a surprising number of winter months too, that water could be heated by the sun. Harnessing the sun's power is an easy way to minimize your household carbon emissions while maximizing your use of a free and renewable supply of energy.

The benefits of "solar thermal collectors", as the rooftop panels that heat water using the sun's energy are called, are numerous: they require very little maintenance; they have virtually no running costs; they usually only take a day to install; and, in most cases, you don't require planning permission.

How do I find a solar thermal collector?

There are now quite a few solar thermal collector manufacturers, but it's worth shopping around. Most companies will send a licensed installer to your home to give you a quote based on your specific needs. Another option is to install a solar thermal collector yourself. Many energy organizations, and even manufacturers themselves, give short courses on DIY installation and maintenance.

How does it work?

■ The solar thermal collector is installed on your rooftop. South-facing roofs pitched at a 35–40° angle are preferable, but not strictly necessary.

■ Heat from the sun is absorbed and retained by insulated tubes. The tubes are designed to work even with minimal sunlight available.

■ Water, directed from the mains pipe, passes through the tubes and is heated up.

■ The hot water is piped into your water storage tank where it is stored until needed.

■ During the summer months, a collector will supply practically all your hot water.

■ Throughout the rest of the year, the collector works alongside your boiler to heat water, but enables you to rely less on your boiler.

NOURISH YOUR SOIL

Although some plants, especially annual weeds, can take root and thrive with hardly any nutrients or water in scrapings of dusty soil, most garden plants need good soil to grow strong and well. Making sure that the soil has a good structure and a supply of nutrients is the most important thing to do before planting, and it will save you having to feed plants in beds and borders once they're established. Plants grown on a healthy diet of naturally enriched soil are less prone to pests and diseases too.

It's useful to know the natural acidity of your soil so that you can grow plants best suited to your conditions and, where needed, make alterations to the soil. Acidity and alkalinity is measured on a pH scale from 0 to 14, 0 being the most acid and 7 being neutral. Certain plants – such as rhododendrons and heathers – thrive on acid soil, but most crops need a neutral to slightly acid soil, with a pH of about 6.5. Adding lime (ideally slow-acting ground limestone) or calcified seaweed in late autumn can raise the pH. Digging in organic matter, especially composted pine needles, can help to neutralize an over-alkaline soil. You can easily check your soil's pH using a soil-testing kit.

Here's a checklist of things you can do to give your plants the best possible growing conditions.

■ **Add bulky organic materials to the soil** These improve the soil's structure, increasing drainage on heavy soils and water retention on light soils, and also feed microscopic creatures,

Digging tips

● Only dig the soil if you need to improve its structure.

● Try not to mix topsoil and subsoil – the subsoil is a different colour to the topsoil.

● Don't dig when the ground is frosted or very wet.

● Try not to walk on the soil, especially when it's wet, as this can compact it and damage the structure. Work from a plank of wood, which spreads your weight, if necessary.

which then make nutrients available to the plants. To improve poor soil, fork plenty of compost or other organic materials into the top 15–20cm (6–8in) of soil. Choose from garden compost, green waste composts, mushroom compost, leafmould, well-rotted manures, straw and hay. Fresh horse or cow manure should be mixed with bedding material such as straw or hay and left to mature for at least a month. This converts the nitrogen and potassium in the manure into forms that the plants can use, and allows any chemical residues to be broken down. Manures and other composts can be bought at garden centres, municipal sites or specialist suppliers, but leafmould and garden compost are easy to make, save waste being sent to landfill, and cost nothing apart from the materials for the bins.

■ **Mulch** Mulching involves putting a generous layer of organic material such as leafmould or compost on the surface of the soil, leaving a space around the stems of the plants. This should be done when the soil is warm and wet. Mulch helps to keep the soil moist and to protect the structure of the soil at the surface. It is eventually incorporated into the topsoil, where it is decomposed by the action of worms and other soil creatures.

■ **Grow green manures** These are fast-growing plants, such as clover (*Trifolium* spp) and *Phacelia tanacetifolia*, that protect bare soil, especially over winter on a vegetable plot, and can be dug in to improve its structure and fertility before planting.

■ **Add organic fertilizers** Organic fertilizers such as bonemeal or rock phosphate are useful when planting new shrubs and trees, or where the soil is poor. Pelleted chicken manure provides nitrogen, phosphates, potash and calcium. Comfrey

What goes in a compost bin?

Yes
● Green matter such as fruit and vegetable scraps, weeds and grass cuttings.

● Brown matter such as leaves of non-coniferous trees and shrubs such as sycamore, ash, poplar, willow, elm, lime and elder, cardboard including cereal packets and egg boxes and woody prunings, etc.

● Organic material such as tea bags, coffee grounds, egg shells, wood ash, wool, straw, pets' bedding, paper towels and newspaper.

No
Meat, fish and cooked food
Weed seeds
Diseased plant material
Disposable nappies and animal faeces
Glossy newsprint
Coal ash

pellets will release trace elements and minerals over several months and can be added to the soil or to potting compost. Once soil has been improved, many plants, especially trees, shrubs and other ornamentals, will not need regular feeding.

How to make garden compost

Compost is made when organic matter is broken down by bacteria. It needs an insulated bin – you can make your own from pieces of wood, or buy a ready-made one in recycled plastic or wood – with a lid or covering, such as a piece of old carpet, to keep the contents warm and the rain out.

A compost bin should be placed on soil so that the soil micro-organisms and composting creatures such as worms can get to work. Fill it with a mixture of green matter – soft materials such as grass clippings, fruit and vegetable peelings and weeds – and tougher, bulkier brown matter, such as woody prunings and cardboard. Keep the heap moist, but not waterlogged. You can make compost in two ways, but for either the material should be cut into small pieces.

For high-speed compost, the heap needs to heat up. The best way to achieve this is to fill the bin up with well-mixed, well-watered materials in one go, and then leave it for a week or two while it heats up. When it starts to cool down, mix it all up to introduce more oxygen, then cover it to let it heat up again. You may need to do this several times, but you should be able to use the dark brown, crumbly composted matter in six to eight weeks. This is an excellent method if you have time to do the turning, and have space for another one or two bins to take your new garden and kitchen waste in the meantime.

The slower, cooler method starts with a 30cm (12in) layer of mixed matter at the bottom of the compost bin; you then add more material as and when you can. Don't put in too much of one thing: mix kitchen peelings with bulkier cardboard or scrunched-up paper, and grass clippings with coarser twigs and stems. If the heap becomes too wet, fork in some bulky woody matter or cardboard. A handful of gardener's lime or ground limestone (wear gloves) stops the heap becoming acidic, which slows down decomposition. Check the bottom of the heap after several months and dig out any dark, well-rotted compost. Then mix up the remaining material, water if necessary and return it to the bin to continue composting.

How to make leafmould

Quantities of leaves are best recycled separately, as they rot down slowly – mainly by the action of fungi. Gather up autumn leaves and water them if they are dry. Pack them into recycled plastic or biodegradable sacks (or a container like a mesh bin), tie the tops, make a few holes in each sack and store out of the way. After one to two years, depending on the leaves, it will be crumbly to the touch and rotted enough to be used as a mulch or soil improver. If left longer, it will decompose further and be fine enough to use in seed-sowing or potting mixes.

MAKE FRESH JUICES

If you have a glut of fruit and vegetables, turn them into healthy, refreshing juices. Apples, carrots and pears are all high in antioxidants and are good sources of vitamin A (carrots) and vitamin C (apples). Apple juice is also known to be cleansing and beneficial to the liver and gall bladder.

Apple, pear & ginger juice
(serves 1)

Apples and pears blend well together, while ginger adds a warming, pungent flavour. This is good to drink if you have indigestion or nausea.

Ingredients

1 apple
1 pear
1 small cube of fresh root ginger

Method

■ Wash the fruit (don't peel or core it) and cut it into small enough chunks to fit in the juice machine feeder.

■ Juice the fruit pieces, together with the ginger.

■ Pour into a glass and drink immediately.

Apple, carrot & beetroot juice

(serves 1)

This fresh juice is a blood-building, nutrient-rich, energy provider.

Ingredients

1 apple
1 carrot, medium
1 beetroot, medium

Method

■ Wash the apple and scrub the carrot and beetroot well. Cut up into small enough chunks to fit in the juice machine feeder.

■ Juice the ingredients and drink immediately.

GROW YOUR OWN VEGETABLES

Depending on how much space you have to spare and how much time you can give to tending them, growing your own vegetables can keep you supplied with ready-to-pick crops all year round. Alternatively, it can offer you the chance to grow some unusual varieties that might be expensive to buy. Either way, the flavour and freshness of what you grow can provide you with the ingredients for a succession of gourmet meals.

If you've never grown vegetables before, it's a good idea to start off with just a few varieties – broad beans, potatoes, spinach beet, chard, courgettes, pumpkins and onions are all pretty straightforward to grow, especially if you buy them as young plants. However, if you want to dedicate several beds or plots to raising vegetables, then it's worth doing some planning first.

Where to grow

Vegetables grow best in a light, open spot in well-drained soil enriched with plenty of organic matter, and with a pH (this measures the acidity of a soil) of around 6.5. A few vegetables, such as beetroot, kale, spinach, radish and calabrese, can cope with light shade, but most crops need at least six hours of full light a day.

The plants also need moisture to enable their rapid growth, so they won't thrive next to a big hedge or tree. If you plan to grow "thirsty" vegetables, such as leafy (spinach, salads, summer cabbage) or fruiting kinds (tomatoes, courgettes, peas, beans), then make sure that there is good access to a water supply. All vegetables also need good air circulation, but in windy sites they may require some protection.

What to grow

It's worth doing some research into the vegetables that you would like to grow and eat. Half-hardy tomatoes, cucumbers, sweetcorn, aubergines and sweet peppers need warm summer temperatures to crop, while cauliflowers are not a good choice for sandy soils. Maincrop vegetables need several months of growing before they are ready to pick, while quick-growing kinds, such as radish, spinach, rocket, spring onions, chard and cut-and-come-again salads, can be harvested in a few weeks and provide pickings before and after maincrops. Long-term vegetables, such as asparagus and rhubarb, are better planted in a plot of their own where they can grow undisturbed.

How to grow

Traditionally, vegetables are grown in long rows with narrow paths for access, but this method tends to be time consuming, and the soil in between the rows can become compacted. Growing vegetables in equal-sized beds, with a generous path around each one, enables you to do all the digging and weeding from the path, and the vegetables to be planted close together. This method gives high returns and is easier to manage. The beds can be made flat on the soil, or raised and contained within a neat edging made of timber planks.

Planning tips

● If you only have a small space for vegetables, or find it difficult to work out a rotation plan with the vegetables you want to grow, stick to just one rule: don't follow crops from a particular family group with ones from the same group, especially if the crop you've just grown has done badly.

● Try to include some vegetables that will provide you with pickings over many weeks. Good crops to choose include leeks, purple-sprouting broccoli and parsnips. Quick-growing crops, such as loose-leaf lettuce, spinach and radish, sown at intervals of a few weeks, give the same effect.

● Make good use of space by following early crops such as potatoes with half-hardy ones such as quick-growing salads, or courgettes and sweetcorn.

Crop rotation

Traditionally, the key to successful vegetable growing, especially the organic way, is crop rotation. This involves planting vegetables in family groups, and ensuring that each group is not grown in the same bed or part of the plot for at least three years.

The main reason for this rotation method is to avoid the build-up of pests and diseases, which attack plants that are botanically related. Crop rotation also helps to keep a balance of nutrients in the soil – legumes, for example, release nitrogen into the soil and so are good crops to grow before brassicas, which need high levels of nitrogen. The rotation system also helps to control weeds: some crops, such as pumpkins and potatoes, have lots of leafy cover that suppresses weeds; others, such as carrots, allow weeds to germinate easily.

Make a plan for a three- or four-year rotation of your beds or plot. Number the beds and allocate a family group to each one. Then decide which vegetables within each group you would like to grow. The carrot and potato families are often grouped together. Work out how many weeks or months each vegetable will be in the ground and choose others to grow before or after, where possible.

Main vegetable families for crop rotation

■ **Brassicas** (*Brassicaceae/Cruciferae*) Some in this group are quick-growing vegetables, such as radish, salad rocket and salad mustard. Most, such as broccoli, Brussels sprouts, cabbage, calabrese, cauliflower, kale, swede and turnip, are in the ground for several months, and it is these crops that need to be rotated.

■ **Legume** (*Leguminosae*) beans, peas, green manures such as clover.

■ **Potato** (*Solanaceae*) potatoes, aubergines, peppers, tomatoes.

■ **Onion** (*Alliaceae*) onions, leeks, garlic, shallots.

■ **Carrot** (*Umbelliferae*) carrots, celeriac, celery, parsnips.

Other vegetables, such as members of the beetroot family (*Chenopodiaceae*) like Swiss chard and spinach beet, members of the daisy family (*Compositae*) such as lettuce, and vegetables such as sweetcorn can be grown in any bed or part of the plot, often before or after the main crop.

Planning a three-year crop rotation scheme

With a rotation scheme, the crops return to their original beds after a break of three to four years.

List all the vegetables you want to grow over a season, and the approximate numbers of plants required for each crop.

Divide the vegetables into groups *(see suggestions, below left)*.

Perennials

If you intend to grow perennial crops, such as asparagus, rhubarb, globe artichokes and Jerusalem artichokes, you should grow them in the same plot for several years, as they take time to establish. Perennial herbs like rosemary can also be grown in this bed.

Rotation group A This group could contain green, leafy brassicas *(see left)*. These plants do best in a slightly alkaline soil (pH 6.5–7), so you may need to apply some lime well before planting.

Rotation group B Legumes, which help to fix nitrogen in the soil, could make up this group *(see left)*. This plot may need general fertilizing early in the growing season.

Rotation group C This group could comprise the potato, onion and carrot families *(see left)*. Of all the groups, this has the highest feeding requirements. Nourish the soil with organic fertilizers, compost or well-rotted manure.

Move the groups from bed to bed each year *(see diagram, right)*. It's a good idea to let the brassica group (A) move into the plot that's just had legumes (B) growing in it, so that there will be plenty of available nitrogen in the soil for these leafy crops.

Year 1

Perennials

Group A

Group B

Group C

Year 2

Perennials

Group C

Group A

Group B

Year 3

Perennials

Group B

Group C

Group A

USE RENEWABLE ENERGY

The simplest way to use renewable energy at home is to switch to a green electricity provider, but if you want to take your green commitment further and the idea of being energy independent appeals, become your own electricity supplier. Micro-generation schemes exist to harness the endless, natural supplies of power from the wind, sun, water and earth.

Those who choose to be energy pioneers are usually looking for more than a quick payback on their energy bills, and it must be said that while off-grid technologies are developing quickly there still isn't an economic argument for generating your own electricity. By opting for small-scale, decentralized electricity generation, however, you'll become part of the building block of a future power grid.

Micro-generation schemes

Before focusing on your supply, minimize your energy demands (check the energy efficiency of your heating, lighting, insulation and electrical appliances).

While some micro-generation schemes come close to fulfilling a household's energy needs, it is prudent to have a fall-back option. Most schemes work in tandem with an existing grid connection, which switches on in times of intermittent supply (as in wind and sun) or at peak usage times. This can also work in your favour – if your demand is low and you produce more electricity than you need, you could sell it back to a main grid.

How to get "unplugged"

Micro wind turbines

Turbines use the wind's forces to turn blades that power a rotor to create electricity. They can be small enough to fit onto a roof and big enough to stand-alone on top of a hill or in a field. Wind speed increases with height, so it's worth checking out the wind speeds of your site before going any further. In urban areas in particular, turbines might not pick up enough wind to be viable.

Solar panels

Photovoltaic solar panels' cells convert the sun's radiation into electricity and, like solar thermal collectors (which heat water), make use of the free source of energy on your roof. A solar panel could provide up to half your electricity needs through the year and avoid creating 650kg (1,433lb) of carbon dioxide.

Ground source heat pumps

Heat from deep underground is extracted through pipes connected to a heat pump, which converts it into high-grade heat for radiators and hot water. You will need to power the heat pump, but you can expect a 4:1 return on the amount of electricity generated.

Hydro power

If you live near a natural water source such as a stream or river, you could use the power from running water to drive a turbine or a water wheel to produce electricity. Depending on the flow rate of the water, micro-hydro sites can generate enough power for all the electrical appliances in a household.

Green energy suppliers

Electricity production is the single biggest contributor to the emissions that cause climate change.

Since 1999, however, UK customers have been able to change their gas or electricity supplier, opening up the market for green energy companies. It's extremely easy to switch to a green energy tariff over the phone or online. Whilst there is no change in the actual energy coming into your home, a proportion of what you pay will be matched by the equivalent amount of energy being fed into the national grid from renewable sources.

PLANT A FRUIT ORCHARD

What could be more enjoyable than an orchard that you've planted yourself? Walking in the dappled shade of blossom-laden fruit trees in spring to the sound of pollinating bees, watching fruits swell on the trees in summer, and picking your own sun-ripened harvest are all experiences not to be missed.

Orchards are special places, and were highly valued in medieval times as gardens in their own right – offering shade, enclosure, tranquillity and, of course, nutritious fruits. With so much of the fruit that we eat nowadays coming from miles (even air miles) away and picked before it is beginning to ripen, you may wonder why we have allowed so many orchards to die out or be felled for intensive agriculture or land development. An orchard offers you the chance to eat your own ripe fruit and choose from an array of wonderful varieties that aren't available in shops. All have their own distinctive flavours and crop successively through the summer and autumn. An orchard is also a magnet for wildlife, especially pollinating insects such as bees and hoverflies, birds such as redwings and fieldfares, butterflies and small mammals, which all feed on fallen fruit. Once the trees mature, countless invertebrates and insects will feed on and live in any dead wood, and birds such as nuthatches, woodpeckers, and tree creepers will nest in hollow trunks.

What you need

Space For a modest-sized orchard, allow enough room to grow at least six standard trees (with trunks at least 1.8m/6ft high) or half-standard trees (with trunks 1.4m/4½ft high). The branches of one tree should not touch any neighbouring branches when fully grown. This means that a vigorous standard apple, such as Blenheim Orange, should be planted at least 9–10m (28–30ft) from its neighbours. You can also grow dwarf trees, often seen planted in crowded rows in commercial orchards, but these do not produce the special sense of place that a traditional orchard filled with tall, airy trees creates. How close you space them depends on the eventual size of the tree, the kind of fruit tree you plant and the local planting patterns (for example, 50 apple trees per acre is common in Somerset).

Well-drained soil: don't plant in soil that is prone to waterlogging.

Shelter Trees need protection from prevailing winds – plant windbreaks if the site is exposed. Don't plant in a frost pocket. In areas that are prone to frost, plant late-flowering varieties.

What to grow

Apples and pears are popular choices, but cherries, plums, damsons, quinces and greengages can all make up your orchard. What you grow depends on what fruits you want to pick for your household, and which varieties are particularly suited to your conditions and the area that you live in. Cherries, for example, do best in sheltered areas where the rainfall is light. They can make majestic trees – up to 12 metres (40ft) tall – and so require plenty of space. All varieties of plum tree flower in spring, so they should be grown in a frost-free site, if possible.

Apple trees can be grown in most places, but before you buy yours do get advice from your local supplier on three things: the rootstock, the most appropriate variety and pollination needs. Apples and pears are grafted onto rootstocks that determine the eventual size of the tree, the age when it starts to fruit and the amount of fruit it can produce. Rootstock M111 will produce a vigorous, wide-spreading standard tree that will start to produce fruit after six years or so. MM106 is used for half-standard trees that bear fruit after four years or so.

A few fruit trees are self-fertile – they can set fruit with their own pollen – but most need one or more other varieties of the same fruit tree, growing no further than 18m (60ft) distance away, to pollinate them. Wind and insects such as bees transfer the pollen from the flowers of one tree to another. Apple trees, for example, are listed in four different pollination groups (A–D) based on their flowering season. Varieties can be pollinated by others in the same pollination group, or in the group just before or after.

Use growers' catalogues to help you make your choice. There are hundreds of varieties to choose from, with different flowering and harvesting times and distinctive flavours and textures, and some are particularly disease-resistant.

Planting & caring for your trees

Orchards certainly don't need to be manicured, but they do need to be looked after, especially in the first few years, in order to produce healthy trees that provide plenty of juicy, vitamin-packed fruits.

Bare-root trees, which are cheaper and easier to plant, should be planted in winter when the tree is dormant, in frost-free soil. Container-grown trees can be planted at any time, but they will establish better if they are planted in winter. If you know how to prune a fruit tree, buy a one-year-old feathered maiden (a tree that has a central stem with a number of lateral branches off it). If not, buy a two- or three-year-old specimen that has already been trained by the grower.

■ **Mark out** the planting area with a cane and measure out the required distance from one tree to the next.

■ **Prepare the soil** before planting, adding plenty of organic matter if the soil is sandy or heavy. Mix some bonemeal into the soil in each planting hole. Put in a short stake on the side of the prevailing wind (although this is not necessary if you are planting a maiden tree), and make sure that the place where the rootstock and grafted stem are joined are positioned well above ground level after planting. Water in the tree and keep well-watered throughout the first year or two – drought stress is a common cause of death in young trees.

Did you know?

Wiltshire has lost 95% of its traditional orchards since the 1960s, Devon has lost 90% and Kent over 80%. Since 1950, 57% of the total orchard area in England has disappeared.

About 6000 varieties of eating and cooking apples have been cultivated in Britain.

Pears are slower to start fruiting than apples, but can produce fruit for up to 300 years.

Researchers have found that eating two apples a day can lower cholesterol levels by up to 10%.

- **Mulch** an area of at least 1m (3ft) in diameter around each tree with well-rotted manure, garden compost, straw or wood chippings, but don't let the mulch touch the trunk. Keep mulching the area, and ensure it is kept weed-free, for the first three to four years (every year if the soil is poor).

- **Fit a tree guard** if there are likely to be grazing animals in the orchard: attach the tree to the stake with a tie made of strong, flexible material.

- **Prune each winter** for the first four or five years, cutting back branches to make a framework of strong, well-spaced branches. Once the tree has developed its framework, all it needs is light pruning in order to take out any dead and diseased wood or crossing branches.

- **Remove all blossom** in the first spring after planting.

- **Feed** with an organic fertilizer in early spring.

- **Encourage natural predators** – blue tits, ladybirds and lacewings will pick off aphids, while underplanting with chives, garlic or tansy will help to deter them. Nectar-rich flowers, such as wildflowers, will attract pollinating insects.

- **Check the tree tie** that is holding the stake every six months or so, and loosen it if it is too tight. Once the tree roots are well-established – usually after one to two years – remove the tie and take out the stake.

Choose your apple trees

How well a tree crops depends on the location and health of the tree. Some, such as Bramley's Seedling and Holstein, can have a less productive season every second year or so. Good apple varieties to try include:

1 Eremont Russet
A classic russet with rough skin, crisp flesh and a sweet flavour. Young trees crop heavily, but mature ones can become irregular.

2 Kidd's Orange Red
A sweet dessert apple, similar to Cox's Orange Pippin, that crops heavily and has quite good resistance to disease. Keeps November to January.

3 Lord Lambourne
A compact tree with medium-sized, red-flushed dessert apples that are sweet and juicy. Crops heavily.

4 Discovery
A bright red early dessert apple with crisp flesh. The blossom is tolerant of frost and the medium-sized fruits keep well.

5 Arthur Turner
A large cooker with a dry texture that is good for baking. Crops heavily.

6 Ashmead's Kernel
One of the best late dessert apples, with crisp flesh and an excellent flavour. Cropping is light. Keeps December to February or March.

7 Pixie
Bears small dessert apples that are yellowish green flushed with red, and which are crisp and juicy. Crops heavily.

8 Sunset
A smallish, cox-like dessert apple that is easy to grown and crops well. Tolerates a moist climate.

9 Winter Gem
A late dessert variety that bears large red-flushed apples with an excellent flavour. Keeps November to February.

Varieties that crop generously

Alkmene (also called Early Windsor)

Arthur Turner (cooker)

Bramley's Seedling (cooker)

Discovery

Egremont Russet

Elstar

Falstaff

GeorgeCave

Kidd's Orange Red

Katy

Kent

Limelight

Lord Derby (cooker)

Lord Lambourne

Red Windsor

Scrumptious

Sunset

Winter Gem

Varieties that store well for several months

Ashmead's Kernel

Bramley's Seedling (cooker)

Claygate Pearmain

Kent

Laxton's Superb

Orleans

Reinette

Pixie

Tydeman's Late Orange

Winter Gem

GROW YOUR OWN RASPBERRIES

Raspberries are some of the most delicious and nutritious summer fruits – they're rich in vitamin C and good for your immune system. Since raspberries are delicate to handle and will spoil in hot conditions or if wet, the varieties that are sold in supermarkets are bred to be firm and long-lasting, and so are not necessarily the most delicious. If you grow your own, you can pick the berries just before eating them, and by planting a range of succulent summer- and autumn-fruiting types you will have a supply of berries from midsummer through to the first frosts. Beg some spare canes from a gardening friend who has good, disease-free plants and you can save yourself even more money.

Raspberry canes carry on cropping for up to ten years. Although they do best in full sun, they can cope with some shade (unlike most other fruits). The small white flowers attract bees and other pollinating insects and the berries make feasts for birds, so either grow some extra canes to allow for bird raids or protect the plants with fine netting.

For the best crops, grow your raspberries in well-drained, well-fed (not chalky) soil, keep them well-mulched and watered and prune them at the right time of year.

How to grow raspberries

The plants are sold as bundles of rooted canes, or rooted in containers. Plant in late winter in soil fed generously with garden compost or well-rotted manure. Most autumn-fruiting varieties have short canes and don't need support, but summer fruiters can reach three metres (10ft) high, so use wooden posts (3m/10ft high) set into the ground at three-metre (10ft) intervals.

Varieties to try

All Gold Autumn-fruiting yellow berries with sweet flavour.

Autumn Bliss Autumn-fruiting large, firm red berries.

Glen Ample Midsummer fruits: large red berries, spine-free stems.

Glen Magna Late summer fruits: large red berries, good disease resistance.

Malling Admiral Late summer fruits: sweet red conical berries, good disease resistance.

Malling Jewel Early summer fruits: firm, dark red berries that ripen slowly. Compact growth.

Tulameen Late summer fruits: large, sweet berries with long picking season.

- Plant the canes in rows, allowing 90cm (36in) between each row. Support the canes with horizontal wires fixed to the posts: fix screws to the posts at 75cm (30in), 1.1m (3½ft) and 1.5m (5ft) intervals from the ground, then attach strong galvanized wire so that it's taut. Plant the canes 40cm (16in) apart, spreading out the roots and firming the backfilled soil.
- Prune the canes to 25cm (10in) once planted. In spring, weed well, mulch with garden compost and add an organic fertilizer.

For summer-fruiting varieties

- These types produce fruit on canes that appeared the previous year. In midsummer, cut down the original cane (there's usually just one per plant) to ground level. Thin out new shoots to about three to six per plant to prevent overcrowding. Do this every summer. Keep well watered and pick berries when ripe.
- In early autumn, cut down the canes that have fruited. Tie in young canes that have grown since midsummer to the wires.
- In winter, add a layer of garden compost to the soil.

For autumn-fruiting varieties

- In summer, tie in the canes but don't cut down the original cane – it will produce fruit later in the year.
- In autumn, pick the ripe berries until the first frosts.
- In winter, cut all the canes down to ground level and protect with a layer of garden compost.

Tips

● Raspberries like cool, moist summers. In hot, dry climates and conditions, autumn-fruiting types will do better.

● Don't let the roots of bare-rooted plants dry out. Plant them as soon as possible.

● Keep the plants weed-free, but hoe carefully as they have shallow roots.

● Hoeing gently round the canes in winter helps to expose overwintering pests, such as the raspberry beetle, so that birds can get at them.

● Thinning the canes to allow the air to circulate will help to protect against diseases.

● Only pick the berries when the weather is dry, as any moisture on the fruit will encourage mould.

● If you have a glut of fruit, freeze the berries.

USE A WOOD-BURNING STOVE

Burning wood can be a very efficient source of energy in the home, but much depends on how the wood is being burned. Open fires, while very cosy on a winter's night, allow most of the heat to vanish up the chimney. A step up is a wood-burning stove. Fuelled by either logs, wood-shavings, sawdust or wood-pellets, it requires a third of the fuel of an open fire and is up to 70 per cent more efficient.

In addition to wood-burning stoves, a range of wood-fuelled boilers are also now available that are as efficient as modern gas boilers – converting over 90 per cent of the fuel into heat. Compared to a conventional boiler, it does take effort to keep wood burners fed, and log boilers need to be refuelled every day, but wood-chip or wood-pellet boilers can be automated to control temperature settings and only need topping up every few days.

Wood fuel

Buying wood fuel, unless you have your own source, will be an ongoing cost, but bought in bulk it is usually less expensive than fossil fuels. It's important to ensure that the wood fuel has a low moisture content: the more moisture it contains, the more inefficiently it burns, and damp wood can emit high levels of pollutants.

As the technologies for using wood as a fuel have advanced, so has the realization that wood is a suitable alternative to fossil fuels. It is widespread, renewable and "carbon neutral" – meaning that when it is burned it releases only the amount of carbon dioxide it absorbed whilst it was growing. Not only that, unlike oil and gas, wood can usually be sourced locally.

GROW FLOWERS FOR CUTTING

In the developed world, especially in Western Europe, North America and Japan, we love to buy cut flowers for our homes, work places, as gifts or for special occasions. Over 50 million roses are given worldwide on Valentine's Day alone. Many of these cut flowers are transported long distances by plane to reach the flower markets as swiftly as possible, and contribute to the problem of increased carbon dioxide emissions.

Cut flowers are also treated with a number of different pesticides, fungicides and fumigants to ensure blemish-free blooms. These chemicals create health problems in many of the countries where the flowers are intensively raised, both for the workforces who may not be properly protected as they work, and in the wider environment where the harmful chemicals can contaminate waterways.

Pure blooms

It's possible to avoid contributing to these problems by growing your own flowers for cutting. With a little planning, you can grow a variety of flowering plants that will provide enough beautiful blooms to fill a vase or two every week from spring through to autumn. By growing your flowers organically – using plenty of organic matter in the soil and as a mulch, and not treating them with chemicals – you can be assured that when you drink in their glorious scents, you're not inhaling a cocktail of toxic chemical residues.

Most flowers for cutting need plenty of sun and fertile, free-draining soil. They can be grown in their own separate bed, or fitted in among other plants, but they shouldn't be planted close to overhanging trees. The most useful flowers to grow for cutting are annuals, biennials or perennials, but bulbs will provide

Picking tips

● Pick flowers early in the day for a longer vase life.

● Cut the stems with a sharp pair of scissors or secateurs – crushing the stems will shorten their vase life.

● Put the flowers in a clean vase with fresh water and refresh after a few days.

● Some flowers, such as gladioli or cleome, make more of an impact as single stems; others are better massed together in a bunch.

Make a simple tonic for your growing plants

Russian comfrey (*Symphytum* x *uplandicum*) makes an excellent organic liquid feed for plants. Wait for a year after planting the comfrey, then cut leaves from April to September. Pile the leaves in a container with a 4–6mm (¼in) wide hole or a tap at the bottom and cover. Draw off the liquid (or let it drip into a jar). Use diluted 1:10 with water if the liquid is thin and brown, 1:20 if it is thick and dark, or store in a bottle for up to a year.

Alternatively, fill an 8 litre (14 pint) bucket with leaves and weigh down with a stone. Add 600ml (1 pint) of rainwater, cover and leave in a warm spot.

After 3–4 weeks, strain the liquid into a bowl or dip a jug into the bucket. Store in a bottle. Dilute 25ml (1fl oz) per litre (1¾ pt) of rainwater.

excellent blooms in spring, especially scented narcissi, hyacinths and lily of the valley. Regularly picking star performers such as sweet peas and cosmos will encourage them to produce yet more blooms.

Sow sweet peas, cerinthe and other hardy annuals early because they tolerate the cold. Half-hardy annuals, such as zinnias, cosmos and antirrhinums, can be sown indoors and planted out once there's no risk of frost. Late-flowering annuals, such as chrysanthemums, can be sown directly in the ground.

Facts on cut flowers

● 85% of the UK's cut flowers are imported. Carnations and roses grown in Colombia travel 8,850 kilometres (5,500 miles) to the UK. Roses, proteas and asters grown in Zimbabwe are transported 8,050 kilometres (5,000 miles).

● A survey of 8,000 Colombian flower workers showed that individuals had been exposed to 127 different pesticides; 20% of these are banned or unregistered in the US.

● Ecuadorian rose producers typically use six fungicides, four insecticides, three nematicides (used to kill nematodes) and several herbicides on their plants.

Take your pick

Spring
Daffodil

Hellebore

Lily of the valley (*Convallaria*)

Solomon's seal (*Polygonatum*)

Tulip

Summer

Acanthus	Love-in-a-mist
Achillea	Peony
Ageratum	Ranunculus
Antirrhinum	Roses (especially scented varieties)
Allium	
Aster	
Ammi	Salvia
Calendula	Scabious
Cerinthe	Sunflower
Cleome	Sweet pea
Cornflower	Zinnia
Cosmos	
Dianthus	
Gaura	
Gladiolus	
Gypsophila	

Autumn
Chrysanthemum

Dahlia

Eremurus

Helenium

Nerine

Rudbeckia

Teasel

PRESERVE FRUIT

Freezing, a modern form of preservation, is neither ecological nor seasonal, but it's the best way to preserve most fruits. As long as they are frozen properly, many fruits will keep their colour, flavour and vitamins, and make a welcome addition to dishes in the winter months. Freezing and using sugar (in fruit recipes) are the most common ways of preserving a crop, although drying fruits or mixing them with a high concentration of alcohol will also stop their natural decay.

Two simple principles govern the process of freezing: the food must be as fresh as possible; and it should be frozen rapidly. Fast-freezing limits the disruption of a food's cell structure – although no matter how fast and efficiently you freeze food its structure will inevitably break down; a frozen raspberry will never look the same as a fresh one. A freezer should operate at -18°C (-0.5°F) or below. At this temperature, the bacteria that spoil food cannot grow.

Most fruits freeze well (with the exception of strawberries), but different procedures suit different fruits. Arrange berries on trays in the freezer and, once frozen, transfer the fruit into rigid containers or plastic bags. Peel and core fruit such as apples and pears, then toss the prepared fruit in a little lemon juice to prevent discolouration before you freeze them. Or pack fruit like plums, peaches and apricots in a cold sugar syrup: make the syrup by boiling 225g (8oz) of sugar with 600ml (1 pint) of water for five minutes. Allow the syrup to cool, then pour over the prepared fruit and freeze. Any fruit can also be frozen as a purée, either cooked or raw. Make all freezer packages as airtight as possible, allowing a little extra space for any liquids to expand, and label them with the contents and date. Frozen fruits are especially good in fruit smoothies, but for other uses thaw the fruit to room temperature first.

A variety of fruit preserves can be made by mixing fruit with sugar. Most jams are made with 500g (1lb) of sugar to every 500g (1lb) of fruit, and should keep for at least a year. This is a good way to use up a glut of fruit, and anything you make yourself is infinitely better than bought produce. However, the high temperatures used in making jam and the amount of sugar required make it a less nutritious form of preservation.

The dehydration technique, which slowly dries fruit by extracting all the moisture, enables fruits to be stored without deteriorating, and is one of the healthiest forms of fruit preservation. If you grow your own fruit, you may prefer to buy a dehydrator. Whether rehydrated or used as they are, dried fruits make an excellent snack food.

Fruits can also be preserved in alcohol – cherries in brandy are particularly good. Simply fill a jar with washed, stoned cherries (use an olive stoner), add a little sugar and cover with brandy. Shake the jar about once a week. The cherries are ready to eat after three months, and make a lovely end to a celebration meal. Pears are also a good choice of fruit to preserve *(see right)*.

Dried apples

If you don't have a dehydrator, try either of the two methods below for drying apples. Peel, core and slice the apples into rings, then put them into a bowl of water mixed with a little lemon juice to prevent them turning brown.

Air-dried Thread the apple rings onto a piece of string and hang the string by an open fire until the apple pieces are completely dried out.

In a conventional oven or an Aga Hang the apple rings on a bamboo stick that measures the width of your oven, or arrange them on a rack. Leave in the oven for about an hour at 49°C/120°F/just under gas 1. Then increase the temperature to 60°C/140°F /gas 1 and leave for three to six hours. If you have an Aga, leave the apple rings for 15 hours on a rack in the bottom cooling oven.

Preserved pears

Pick the best pears from your harvest. If you want to peel, halve and core the pears, quickly blanch them afterwards in boiling water for two minutes, then put them in cold water.

In a thick-bottomed pan add 300g (10oz) of unrefined sugar to 1 litre (1¾ pints) of water and boil for five minutes. Meanwhile, put the fruit into a large sterilized, heat-resistant jar, leaving a gap of 2cm (¾in) below the rim. When the syrup is ready, pour it over the pears until they are completely covered.

Loosely close the jar without sealing it and place it on a wooden trivet in a pan of boiling water. Simmer the jar for up to 30 minutes, or until the pears are cooked. Then seal the jar shut, allow to cool and store in a cool, dry place.

KEEP A FEW GEESE

Keeping geese seems to have gone a little out of fashion, which is perhaps surprising, as they produce delicious free-range eggs and premium organic meat, will largely look after themselves and are effective burglar alarms.

Geese are considered low-maintenance livestock, needing little additional feeding so long as grass or other grazing is plentiful; they are natural lawn mowers. As long as they have enough space, they'll be happy. Start by buying a goose and a gander; they will form a bond that will last their lifetime. If you want geese for both eggs and meat, buy at least two geese and one gander so that if you slaughter one goose, the other won't be left alone.

Geese have exceptional eyesight and a wide field of vision. Some breeds can be extremely vocal if they observe something or somebody unfamiliar or sense a perceived threat. As a result, they are occasionally used to guard whisky warehouses and even military installations. If you keep geese for security purposes, a highly-strung light breed such as the Chinese goose is a good choice. Before buying any geese, it's worth checking that your neighbours will not object, and also check with your local council.

Goose eggs

The laying season for geese starts in midwinter and continues until midsummer. A single goose can lay up to 80 eggs a year, which is remarkable given that the eggs weigh 200 grams (8oz) each. Remove the eggs as soon as possible, but take care, as geese can be protective of their clutch. The eggs should be stored in a cool, draught-free place in clean egg trays.

Choose your geese

Geese are grouped into three types – light, medium and heavy breeds – based on their size and weight. You should select a breed according to whether you want it for eggs or meat: in general, the heavier breeds lay fewer eggs, but all of the breeds may be used for meat. The medium and light breeds are the most practical geese to keep.

If you want to breed geese for the table, heavy breeds like the Toulouse and White Embden, which are twice as big as the other breeds, provide an enormous 11kg (24lb) or more of meat, while medium breeds, such as the Grey Back and American Buff, tend to weigh about 6.5–9kg (14–20lb). Light breeds, such as the Chinese and Pilgrim geese, produce a 4.5–6.5kg (10–14lb) table bird; two small birds are often better-tasting than one large goose. Geese take up to 30 weeks to mature.

Signs of good health in a goose

- Dry nostrils.
- Bright eyes with no soreness.
- Clean, shiny feathers.
- Good weight and musculature for age.
- Clean vent (rear-end) feathers with no smell.
- Straight toes and undamaged webs.
- Alert and active bird with no sign of lameness.

Geese are generally hardy, and most ailments are caused by poor husbandry. Stay aware of any news on avian flu and contact Defra for advice.

Grey Back
Also known as the "pied" or "spot" goose. Like the American Buff, an average egg-layer that produces tasty meat. Calm, docile and suited to a small home flock.

American Buff
An ideal medium breed. Not as good a layer as smaller breeds, but produces tasty meat for roasting. Calm, docile and well-suited to a small home flock.

Chinese
A light, intelligent breed, either white with an orange knob and bill, or fawn. Lays an impressive 60 eggs a year, and makes a fierce guard.

Pilgrim
A light and practical breed that is ideal for a smallholding. The male is all white and the female mainly grey. Lays approximately 20 eggs a year.

Getting started

Geese are more self-sufficient than ducks and like to roam freely. They are not fussy birds and, as long as they have fresh water, mixed corn, grit, and a large supply of grass, they need little else. Their main need is to be protected from foxes and vermin at night.

Geese need to be taught where their home is; if your new arrivals are not used to a goose house, keep them penned up in their house with a large outdoor mesh run for a few days to get them accustomed to their new surroundings. If you don't have a fox-proof fence around the field or area where your geese will roam, shut them in their house every night. A laying goose needs to feel that she is safe and dry in her house, so clean out the shed and the run (if you have one) as often as possible, as geese can be messy.

If grass and other grazing is plentiful, your geese won't need extra feeding for long periods of the year. Allow your geese to forage for their own food: 80 per cent of their food will come from grass and weeds. If sufficient natural food is not available, provide chopped greens (cabbage leaves, kale and lettuces) and cereals (whole grains). Make sure that the geese always have mixed grit freely available. To fatten geese quickly for eating, feed them on ground barley and wheat in equal amounts, twice daily, for three weeks. You can also feed up laying geese in midwinter just before they start to lay.

Geese need access to some water, and a clean pond with proper drainage is ideal. However, unlike ducks, a water trough that is deep enough to allow the geese to dip their heads in and bathe (to avoid skin parasites and sore eyes) will be an adequate substitute. In summer, you should ensure that your geese have plenty of shade, as they are prone to sunstroke.

A goose keeper's kit

1 Fresh water

As with all livestock, geese need access to supplies of fresh water. If you don't have a pond and use a water trough instead, ensure that it is deep enough for the geese to dip their heads.

2 Open pasture

Geese are grazing animals, so allow them as much open space as you can. If the grass and weeds are plentiful, they will only need a small amount of supplementary feeding. Confining geese in a small area will damage the grass.

3 Feed trough

Use a feed trough when you feed your geese whole grains and chopped greens, otherwise the geese will trample and waste their food.

4 Goose house

Each goose needs at least 120sq cm (4sq ft) of sleeping space in the house, which can be as simple or as elaborate as you like, as long as it protects the birds from predators at night. A shuttered entrance will help to keep the birds securely inside. The floor should always be kept clean and dry.

5 Informal nest box

Laying geese are not fussy about where they lay their eggs, as long as they have a dry, secure nest. Fill an old crate with straw and leave it in a sheltered corner.

6 Upright nest box

Alternatively, you can stand a nest box on its side, line it with straw and position it so that it is sheltered from wind, rain and sun.

MAKE SUMMER FRUIT JAMS

Home-made jams on a breakfast table are a cheering sight, and a sweet reminder of the delectable tastes of summer fruits. Making jam is a surprisingly straightforward process, and the filled jars make lovely gifts if you cover the sealed lids with circles of pretty fabric.

Making jam at home doesn't require specialist equipment, but it's as well to check that you have a suitable pan with a thick base (there's no need for a lid when making jam). If you want to invest in a preserving pan, buy a heavy-gauge pan. Ideally, preserving jars are best for both jams and chutneys, as they have proper lids that seal down, but glass jars with screw-top lids work just as well. Circles of waxed paper placed (wax-side down) over the top of the jam can also provide a seal. Use firm rather than over-ripe fruit, and wash the fruit several times in cold water before you use it.

Testing for the setting point

Spoon a small amount of the boiling jam onto a plate, pop the plate into the fridge and allow to cool. The jam is ready if the sample forms a skin that is firm enough to wrinkle when you push it with your fingertip. If the sample remains completely fluid, continue to boil the jam for a few minutes, then re-test.

Sterilizing jars & lids

Jars for jams and pickles should always be scrupulously clean. Wash jars well and place in a moderate oven for five minutes to sterilize them.

Blackcurrant jam

(Makes 2.2kg/5lb)

Ingredients

1kg (2½lb) fresh blackcurrants, washed

570ml (1 pint) water

2kg (4lb) unrefined organic sugar

Method

■ Put the fruit and water into a thick-bottomed pan. Simmer gently for 30 minutes. Add a little extra water if needed to stop the mixture burning.

■ Add the sugar and stir until dissolved. Boil rapidly for 10–15 minutes.

■ Test for the setting point, take the pan off the heat, then spoon into jars and seal.

Variation
Redcurrant jam

Use 1kg (2½lb) fresh redcurrants.

Strawberry jam

(Makes 2.2kg/5lb)

Ingredients

1.3kg (3lb) fresh strawberries, hulled and washed

Juice of 2 lemons

1.3kg (3lb) unrefined organic sugar

Method

■ Cook the fruit and juice in a thick-bottomed pan over a low heat until the juices run (10–15 mins).

■ Add the sugar and stir until dissolved. Bring to the boil and cook rapidly for 15 minutes.

■ Test for the setting point, then spoon into jars and seal.

Variation
Strawberry & lime jam

Use the juice of 1 lemon and 2 limes. Add the zest of 2 limes before putting the jam into jars.

GROW PLANTS TO ATTRACT WILDLIFE

If you have some soil, flowering plants and shrubs, a tree or two and a bird bath or a small pond, then you'll have wildlife in your garden – and probably in much greater quantities than you realise.

Much wildlife will be tiny – some even microscopic – but these creatures form the base of the food chain that feeds the mammals, birds and amphibians that increasingly rely on gardens for their survival; many insects, such as bumblebees and moths, are in decline.

Providing for beneficial insects that pollinate as they travel around the garden, fly from one garden to the next or feed on garden pests such as aphids (one hoverfly larva can devour around 1,000 aphids in its lifetime) is one of the most helpful ways to support wildlife. Flowers, for example, provide nectar and pollen, which are essential for insects such as butterflies, bees, hoverflies and lacewings to feed on. Both native and non-native plants can provide this, but they must have flower structures that allow the insects to get at the nectar and pollen.

By providing a range of different areas to feed, shelter and breed in, and water to drink, you will make your garden an even better refuge for wildlife. You'll be rewarded with the pleasure of watching or hearing these wild creatures feed, drink and move about.

Try to include as many of the following as you can in your garden or plot of land:

Trees No matter how small or large, trees provide song posts and shelter for birds. Mature trees can make excellent nest sites for birds such as treecreepers, tits and woodpeckers. Some species, especially native trees, also harbour huge numbers of insects and invertebrates. Willows, for example, are an important plant food for moths which, in turn, attract bats.

Ground cover Many creatures, such as ground beetles and centipedes, need the dark, moist conditions that exist underneath groundcover plants or plant material to survive. Frogs and toads can find shelter under low-growing plants too.

Shrubs Along with trees, shrubs provide natural windbreaks, creating sheltered areas that are needed by insects such as butterflies and bees. The leaves, flowers, berries, fruit and seeds of shrubs also provide food for many creatures.

Flowering plants Plan to have plants in flower from early until late in the growing season. Early foragers such as bees, and late feeders such as butterflies, particularly need help. Avoid double flowers, multi-petalled forms or hybrid cultivars that do not produce pollen or nectar.

Flowers from two families, Apiaceae and Asteraceae, are good to plant: Apiaceae (includes umbellifers such as fennel and dill) produce huge amounts of nectar over a short period of time; Asteraceae (daisy-like flowers including asters and sunflowers) produce smaller amounts over a long period.

Climbing plants Climbers provide homes for insects and small mammals, and nest sites for small birds. By growing these plants up bare fences or walls you can, from a wildlife point of view, increase the size of your garden.

Berries & seeds By planting species that bear berries and fruits, and leaving seed-bearing stems standing at the end of the growing season, you will help birds and small mammals survive the winter months when their natural food sources are greatly reduced. Standing stems also provide hibernation sites for insects.

Grass Long grass makes an excellent habitat for insects such as damselflies, grasshoppers and other small creatures, while birds such as starlings and blackbirds will hunt for invertebrates in grass. Some butterflies also lay their eggs in grasses. If you have a lawn, leave a section of it uncut as a natural habitat for these different creatures.

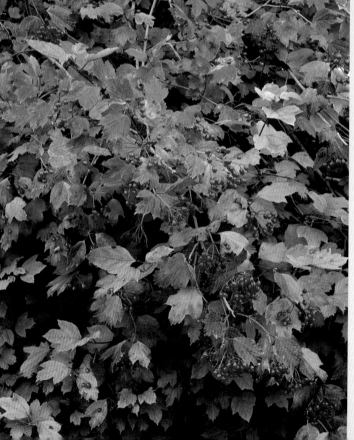

Hedges Hedges, especially those composed of native species such as hawthorn, guelder rose, hazel and beech, create shelter and homes for a wide number of creatures. Hedges also create corridors for wildlife to move from one area to another in safety.

Plants that provide early pollen and nectar

■ Trees such as willow *(Salix caprea)*, hazel *(Coryllus avellana)*, mimosa.

■ Shrubs such as *Viburnum tinus*, Mahonia, bramble.

■ Bulbs such as crocus, grape hyacinth *(Muscari)*, snowdrop *(Gallanthus)*.

■ Flowers such as Forget-me-not *(Myosotis)*, primrose *(Primula)*, wallflower *(Cheiranthus)*.

Plants that provide late pollen and nectar

■ Shrubs such as *Buddleja,* heather *(Calluna vulgaris)* and tree ivy *(Hedera helix* 'Arborescens's*)*.

■ Flowering plants such as ivy *(Hedera)*, sedum *(Sedum* species), Michaelmas daisy *(Aster* species), coneflower *(Echinacea* species), rudbeckia *(Rudbeckia* species), heather *(Calluna* and *Erica* species), fennel *(Foeniculum vulgare)*.

Other ways that you can make your garden or plot of land attractive to wildlife

■ Leave a few piles of dead wood on the ground, which will be used by a wide variety of invertebrates, and serve as a shelter for frogs, toads and newts.

■ Leave out food for birds, especially in winter and spring.

■ Make a pond with shallow edges, and grow some native plants in and around it.

■ Put up nest boxes for birds, bats and owls.

■ Make nesting sites for solitary bees by drilling holes of different dimensions in wood.

■ Put up homes for overwintering insects, such as ladybirds and lacewings.

Did you know?

● It's good news for plants to have birds eating their berries, as the birds drop or excrete the seeds and so enable the plants to spread. Birds are attracted to bright red yew berries, for example. They swallow the fruit, but then spit out the seed, which has a poisonous (and bad-tasting) coating.

● Fennel *(Foeniculum vulgare)* is a gardener's friend: it can attract around 500 species of insect, more than half of them devourers of pests such as aphids and caterpillars.

● In the UK, the native oak *(Quercus robur)* supports 284 species of insect; the non-native horse chestnut *(Aesculus hippocastanum)* supports just four species.

MAKE BERRY LOLLIES & FRUIT COMPOTE

Soft fruits like berries won't keep for long after they've been picked, so one of the best ways to preserve their heavenly juices and sweet summer taste is to turn them into ice lollies or compote, which can also be frozen. The compote is delicious with ice cream, in a pie or as the basis of a summer pudding.

Berry lollies

Ingredients

250g (8oz) caster sugar

250ml (8fl oz) water

500g (1lb) fresh berries – either raspberries, strawberries or blackberries, washed

50ml (2fl oz) fresh lemon juice

Method

■ Make a sugar syrup first: put the sugar and water in a thick-bottomed saucepan. Place the pan over a low heat and stir the mixture with a wooden spoon until the sugar has dissolved.

■ Turn up the heat and bring the syrup to a steady boil for five minutes. Then turn off the heat and allow the syrup to cool.

■ Purée the berries by passing them through a sieve, which will also remove all the seeds.

■ Mix the berry purée with the lemon juice and sugar syrup. Taste the mixture and if you think that it needs to be sweeter, stir in a little sifted icing sugar. If you prefer the taste to be a little sharper, add some more lemon juice.

■ Pour the mixture into ice lolly moulds, slot an ice cream stick into each mould and freeze the lollies until required.

Variation

Blackcurrant, gooseberry or rhubarb lollies

You can also make fruit lollies using blackcurrants, gooseberries and rhubarb, but you need to cook the fruit first.

■ Place 1kg (2lb 4oz) of washed fruit in a pan, barely cover the fruit with water and add 250g (9oz) of caster sugar.

■ Stir over a low heat until the sugar has dissolved, then simmer for about five minutes until the fruit is completely tender.

■ Leave to cool for a few minutes, then pour the fruit and juices into a large nylon sieve set over a jug.

■ Push the fruit through the sieve to create a smooth purée.

■ Taste the purée and, if it needs it, stir in a little sifted icing sugar. Pour into moulds, push in the ice cream sticks and freeze.

Forest fruit compote

Ingredients
65g (2½oz) redcurrants or blackcurrants
120g (4½oz) blackberries
120g (4½oz) raspberries
100–150g (4–5oz) caster sugar
A dash of lemon juice

Method
■ Put all the berries in a small bowl, add the sugar and leave to macerate for at least 1 hour.

■ Add the lemon juice and set aside to be used, or freeze in sealed containers until required.

GROW COMPANION PLANTS

When European monks planted clumps of chives under roses in their walled gardens in medieval times, the term "companion planting" hadn't yet been coined, but they were certainly practising it: deliberately growing a particular plant because of its effect on another plant. In this case, the chives, probably due to their pungent oils, were thought to keep aphids away from the roses and to keep diseases like blackspot at bay.

Common pests that companion plants will help to repel

Blackfly

Carrot fly

Flea beetles

Greenfly

Leafhoppers

Thrips

Whitefly

Wireworms

Organic gardeners today can make use of lots of companion plants to protect vulnerable crops and to fertilize the soil. Although there is scientific evidence for only some of these practices, it's well worth giving them a try, both in the vegetable bed or garden and in your flower borders, as it helps gardeners understand the natural rhythms of a planted garden. It's also inexpensive – the price of a packet of seeds – if you grow the plants yourself.

There are various ways in which plants can be good companions.
Providing shelter and shade In temperate gardens, strong winds can kill off certain plants by buffeting them and chilling the air temperature by as much as 10°C (15-20°F), especially in winter and early spring when the young plants are beginning to grow new shoots.

The best kind of shelter for vulnerable plants is other plants, such as those suitable for hedging and trees, which will filter the wind but not block it completely (a solid windbreak creates

a void which draws down the wind in eddies, creating even worse damage). Other plants, such as deciduous trees, create the shade that woodland species such as ferns need to thrive.

Attracting beneficial insects While there are some insects that attack the plants in the garden, there's an army of other insects that are beneficial, either because they pollinate plants (which is especially useful for certain fruits and vegetables) or they prey on pests such as aphids. Flowering plants with accessible supplies of nectar and pollen – for example, tubular-shaped flowers such as foxgloves for long-tongued butterflies and bumblebees, and flat, open flowers such as asters for ladybirds and lacewings – will provide food for these insects. By making sure that you have a succession of these flowers (they should be single flowers, not doubles or multi-petalled), from early spring onwards, you are likely to have a healthy population of helpful insects in your garden or vegetable plot throughout the growing season.

Confusing and repelling pests Certain plants seem to keep pests away from their target plants by confusing them. Pot marigolds (*Calendula*) are useful at the base of vegetables such as tomatoes and cucumbers as they draw whitefly away from the crops, possibly because of their bright petals. In the same way nasturtiums act like a beacon for blackfly and cabbage caterpillars. Mustard *(Brassica hirta)* is a useful plant to grow with potatoes, as wireworms are attracted to its roots. Many insects recognise their food by its smell, so growing a strongly aromatic plant such as mint, sage, onion or parsley close to carrots may confuse the carrot fly so that it doesn't find its preferred plant. French marigolds (*Tagetes*) produce a strong smell that seems to keep aphids away, while chives and garlic, which are rich in volatile oils, also seem to repel insects such as leafhoppers and aphids.

Providing nutrients Certain plants benefit others by making nutrients accessible to them. Beans and other legumes convert nitrogen gas from the air into a form they can use in their roots, and when they die this valuable plant nutrient is released into the soil. Comfrey and borage provide extra potassium and calcium for neighbouring plants, while parsley seems to make tomatoes more vigorous, and asparagus helps potato plants to grow well.

Super companions

1 Calendula *(C. officinallis)*
Provides nectar and pollen for insects until late autumn and attracts whitefly and other pests.

2 Candytuft *(Iberis umbellata)*
Long-flowering annual that provides nectar and pollen for insects and, if planted under brassicas, reduces flea beetles.

3 Onion *(Allium cepa)*
Interplanted with carrots, it may help to reduce carrot fly and thrips.

4 Marigold *(Tagetes)*
Its strong smell may help to repel aphids, such as greenfly and blackfly.

5 Yarrow *(Achillea millefolium)*
Attracts predatory wasps, ladybirds and hoverflies, and can improve vigour in neighbouring plants.

6 Nasturtium *(N. officinale)*
Helps to deflect aphids from broccoli and squash and acts as a decoy near cabbages.

7 Chives *(Allium schoenoprasum)*
Attracts beneficial insects and may help to repel aphids.

8 Garlic *(Allium sativum)*
Can confuse pests such as leafhoppers, aphids and carrot fly.

9 Poached egg plant *(Limnanthes douglasii)*
Long-flowering annual that provides nectar and pollen for insects.

KEEP HONEY BEES

Bees exist in almost every part of the world, and are one of the most useful of all insects – not only is their honey highly prized and their beeswax useful, they also play a crucial role in pollinating plants, encouraging flowers to bloom for longer and generating richer crops of fruit and vegetables.

There are about 20,000 species of bees, but it is only honey bees that make honey and wax in large amounts. Honey bees (workers, drones and queens) are fascinating creatures: they have their own social system and complex behavioural patterns, which we are only just beginning to understand. Working with a community of bees offers an absorbing and unique insight into the annual cycles and workings of the natural world.

The beekeeper's calendar

Before you start keeping bees, it's important to understand the annual life cycle of bees and the tasks you will need to perform as a beekeeper.

Early spring The queen bee starts to lay eggs in February. The honey stores in the hive will be running low after the winter because – despite the emergence of spring flowers – nectar and pollen are in very short supply. Fill the bees' feeder with sugar syrup, if necessary, to supplement the natural nectar around.

Late spring There's a rapid increase in the brood. The bees fly on fine warm days to gather nectar and pollen from the early blossoms. This is the time to make the removable "supers" (frames inside the hive that contain chambers where the honey is stored), and fix in place the queen excluder, which prevents the queen from laying eggs in the honey store.

Summer Pollen and nectar are in abundant supply for the bees. This is the busiest season for a beekeeper, as the hive needs to be checked weekly and boxes of supers added and removed as necessary. The main skill of beekeeping is to prevent "swarming" – when a new queen leaves the hive, taking possibly more than half of the colony's bees with her. This happens when the bees detect that the hive is becoming too cramped and cells for new queens form. These cells are long and pointed compared to normal cells, and are often hidden in corners and difficult to find. Any queen cups (empty cells built in preparation for queen larvae) and cells you find should be destroyed by squashing them with a hive tool. By late summer the supers are full of honey; watch out for wasps trying to rob the hive.

Autumn The bees are past swarming by this time, and the beekeeper can begin to relax and harvest the honey. Once you have removed the honey store and effectively taken away the bees' winter larder, feed them with sugar syrup. It's also important to protect your hive from the Varroa mite, which carries a virus: remove the supers and suspend two medicated plastic strips in the brood frame. The strips contain chemicals that are slowly released into the hive and kill the mites. Remove the strips after six weeks; if you do detect an infection, treatment is possible, so seek professional advice.

Winter After collecting the last of the autumn nectar, the bees remain in the hive. The drones are expelled from the hive to die in the cold, as they are no longer useful and the honey store is needed for the queen and the workers. The bees collect in a mass in the centre of the hive, close to their food supply. Once the bees have shut up shop for the winter, don't disturb them.

Buy your bees

Spring is the time to acquire your bees. Your local beekeeping society or group will be happy to give advice and supply you with the equipment and bees: it's best to purchase a "nucleus" of bees (a queen and worker bees) from an experienced beekeeper or specialist supplier. The colony will have a frame containing a single queen, worker bees, cells of eggs and developing grubs. The queen is larger than the workers, with a more pointed rear end. She has a sting, but will only use it on a rival queen. To identify the queen, carefully mark a coloured dot, using a felt tip pen, on her head.

Place the queen in a small plastic container in the brood chamber (where she lays her eggs in the frames) and seal the container with a boiled sweet. The worker bees become accustomed to the queen's smell in the time that it takes them to eat the sweet. They will then accept her and she will start to lay eggs. Feed the new colony with sugar syrup for the first week until they build up their own honey store.

Getting started

There are two main types of hive: the National Hive (a single-walled structure that is light and easy to relocate) and the WBC (the traditional design with double walls that keep bees cool in summer and warm in winter). To avoid disease, it's best to begin with a new hive, but secondhand hives can be used, provided they are thoroughly cleaned and repaired where necessary. If you purchase a new hive, you'll need to make your own frames, or "supers", and repair and maintain the hive later on, so it's important to have a basic understanding of woodwork skills. The hive should be located in a warm, sheltered position facing south, away from overhanging trees. The bees prefer to have a clear flight path into and out of the hive, as they enter and leave at approximately a 60-degree angle. To prevent the base of the hive from rotting, and for ease of access, build a brick platform on which to stand the hive.

Making a frame from a kit

Don't use secondhand frames – they can carry disease. Save money by making your own frames, or use kits: the precut ends should slot easily together.

Slot the thin wax sheet of foundation, which is stamped with a hexagonal pattern that acts as a guide for the bees to construct their honey, into the sides of the frame.

Hammer in the pins to fix the lower edge of the frame. The fixing needs to be firm or the frame will come apart when fully laden with the bees' honey.

Your hive should always be well maintained and cared for. A broken hive will be harder to disassemble smoothly (and will upset the bees), and may allow "robbers", such as wasps and other bees, to find their way in and steal honey. Worse still, it may even result in your bees moving out of their home.

A new colony won't produce a significant yield of honey in its first year, but an established hive can produce up to 27kg (60lb) of honey in a good year. The type of honey produced depends on the availability of flowers and foliage in the area (clear honey, for example, is produced by bees collecting nectar from garden flowers). It's possible to produce speciality honey, such as heather, clover or orange blossom, from a single source of nectar by placing the hive out of range of all other nectar sources. This can be difficult to achieve, so if you are new to beekeeping a blended honey may be the best option.

A beekeeper's kit

You can purchase a hive, suit, tools and honey extractor from specialist suppliers or through your local beekeeping society. Keep all your equipment in good condition.

Clothing
- A good-quality bee suit, helmet and veil.
- Long rubber or leather gloves and boots. Ideally, all clothing should be white, a colour that bees find calming.

Smoker & other tools
- Use a smoker before opening the hive: after three minutes, the bees become drowsy and fill their sacks with honey, believing that there is a nearby fire and danger is ahead. With full honey sacks, it's then hard for them to use their stings. Burn dry hay or grass cuttings to produce the smoke (or some beekeepers use strips of hessian sacking, as it burns for longer).
- A soft brush to gently remove the bees from the honey frames.
- A feeder to supplement the bees' diet with sugar syrup.
- A hive tool, a flat piece of metal with a curved end, to open the hive and to loosen supers that have become stuck together.

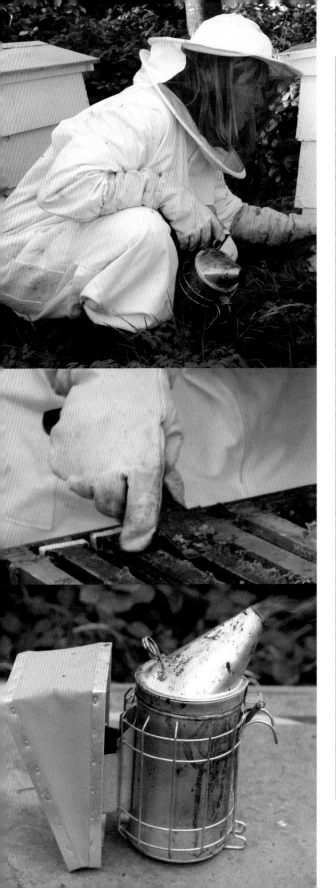

Harvesting honey

Part the bees from their honey by placing an "extra crown board", fitted with a bee escape, between the brood box and the super (where the honey is). This allows the bees to go into the brood chamber (where the queen lays her eggs), but not to return to the super. Allow at least 24 hours to clear a hive; by the next day, the majority of your bees will be safe in the brood chamber.

Smoke the hive and remove the roof and crown board underneath. Remove the supers to a safe place where the bees can't access them. A hive will need 10–14kg (20–30lb) of honey to survive the winter, so don't take all the harvest. Slow, deliberate movements won't disturb the bees as much as quick movements will (bees can sense uncertainty or panic and won't respond positively). You can estimate how much honey there is as you lift each frame; if it doesn't weigh much, it's better left for the bees. Lightly brush off any bees down into the hive.

Slice off the worker bees' wax caps (which seal the honey inside the cells) with a warmed knife.

Place the supers in a honey extractor, a centrifugal separator that works like a spin-dryer, throwing the honey off the frames.

Strain the honey through a honey strainer for 24 hours, then decant into clean, sterilized jars and seal.

The beeswax can be used in candles, polishes and other products. The empty frames can be left out by the hive for the bees to clean up.

CHOOSE A GREEN CHRISTMAS TREE

For many of us, an intrinsic part of our Christmas celebrations involves putting up and decorating a conifer tree, and enjoying the resiny smell of its needles and the cheerful sight of the decorated branches for several weeks in the middle of winter. Although we are beginning to understand the importance of recycling our cut trees – they can be reduced to chippings and put back into the environment as mulch, path surfacing, and in soil improvers – a vast number of Christmas trees are still sent to landfill sites.

There are two ways of making your Christmas tree as "green" as possible: either buy a living tree, and after Christmas plant it in the garden as a ornamental tree or keep it in its pot outside to get a second chance of using it the following Christmas; or buy a cut tree that has been grown sustainably (look for a Christmas tree growers' association label or logo) – preferably from a local grower to minimize transport miles – and ensure that the tree is recycled after you've used it. Many councils arrange special recycling facilities for trees after Christmas, and growers' associations will take back and recycle any tree purchased from them.

Some Christmas tree conifers can grow to great heights – the Nordman fir *(Abies nordmanniana)* can reach 40 metres (131ft) – so if you plan to plant yours outside, check on its eventual height first. Any container-grown conifer will look suitably Christmassy and, if you buy a dwarf conifer, you should be able to keep it in a pot for several years if you feed, water and re-pot it regularly. Some Christmas tree growers offer more unusual varieties, such as the Korean Fir *(Abies koreana)*, which has purple cones and grows to ten metres (30ft), or the Colorado Blue spruce *(Picea pungens* 'Glauca'), which grows to 24 metres (80ft).

How to look after a living tree

● Buy a container-grown tree, offered at a maximum height of about 1.5m (5ft), and soak it well before bringing it into the house.

● Keep the tree away from direct heat, such as radiators or open fires, and water regularly, just as for most house plants.

● Don't keep the tree indoors for more than a month, as the warmth and artificial lights of your home can make the tree break dormancy and start to put on new growth. Putting the tree outside at that point could then kill it.

● After Christmas, take the tree outdoors. Either re-pot it in early spring into a larger container (use a bark-based coarse organic compost with some slow-release organic fertilizer, such as comfrey pellets, and keep it well watered) or plant it into the ground in well-drained soil that's not frosted. Make the planting hole a generous size, add some bonemeal and keep the tree well watered for the first couple of years.

DESIGN A HERB GARDEN

Herbs were among the earliest plants grown, mainly for their medicinal uses, by gardeners. Today, they are still really satisfying plants to grow. They don't take up much room, so you can grow many different kinds in a small space, and they can provide you with year-round fresh leaves for the kitchen and home remedies. Many of them are wonderfully aromatic, and have striking foliage and flowers. Growing herbs organically will also ensure that any you pick will be free from harmful chemicals.

You can grow herbs in a variety of ways: in gaps in gravel or between paving slabs; in a collection of individual pots; grouped together in a ceramic sink; among the other flowering plants in beds or borders, as edging along paths; or in their own designated beds. The size, location and style of your garden will to some extent dictate how you grow herbs, but the first thing you need to decide is what you want to grow your herbs for.

Ask yourself:
- Do you mainly want to use herbs in the kitchen and in remedies?
- Do you want them to provide a sensory part of the garden, full of scent and attracting pollinating insects such as bees?
- To create a decorative feature, such as a grid of equal-sized beds divided by crisp gravel paths, edged with bricks, tiles or wood, and filled with a counterpane of green, grey, purple, yellow and silver foliage?
- Or maybe you want an all-purpose herb area, which gives you elements of all these things?

Next, consider some practicalities:

Eventual height and spread Check how big the plants will eventually grow, so that you can be sure they will fit in the space allocated. Think about including a mixture of evergreens and annuals, and tall and low plants. Containing the beds in some way – whether with clipped plants or hard materials – will make them easier to manage.

Growing conditions Many herbs originally grew wild in the Mediterranean, and so prefer dry, well-drained sunny sites – although some, such as parsley and mint, do better if shaded from the midday sun. Herbs such as basil are tender annuals, while mint and rosemary are hardy evergreens.

Choice of herbs What will you enjoy looking at or cooking with?

Site If you want to cook with herbs, try to position them close to the kitchen door; if you want to make a feature, choose a spot where the herbs will not be obscured by a more dominant feature. A bed of up to 1.2m (4ft) wide will allow you to care for the plants and pick their leaves from the path.

Herb beds

Traditionally, herbs were grown in rectangular beds with paths in between, but they grow well in "wheels" divided into segments, each planted with a single variety, or ovals, ellipses, triangles and squares. Visit herb gardens for inspiration, then draw up your plan.

Formal designs Often geometric and edged with tightly clipped plants such as box. They often make use of repeat plantings of evergreens, such as cotton lavender, thyme, hyssop or hedge germander, to make strong, symmetrical patterns. These herb gardens are high maintenance, as they need regular clipping and very precise planting.

Semi-formal designs Usually make use of clipped box edging filled with looser plantings of herbaceous herbs.

Informal designs Appear loose and unplanned, but need to be worked out before planting so that there's a balance of large and smaller species, and an attractive mix of colours.

Herbs for the kitchen

Basil *(Ocimum)*

Bay *(Laurus nobilis)*

Chives *(Allium schoenoprasum)*

Dill *(Anethum graveolens)*

Fennel *(Foeniculum vulgare)*

French tarragon *(Artemisia dracunculus)*

Marjoram *(Origanum vulgare)*

Mint *(Mentha)*

Parsley *(Petroselinum crispum)*

Rosemary *(Rosmarinus officinalis)*

Sage *(Salvia officinalis)*

Salad burnet *(Sanguisorba minor)*

Sweet marjoram *(Origanum majorana)*

Thyme *(Thymus vulgaris)*

Winter savory *(Satureja montana)*

Aromatic herbs

Basil *(Ocimum)*

Catnip *(Nepeta)*

Coriander *(Coriandrum sativum)*

Cotton lavender *(Santolina)*

Curry plant *(Helichrysum italicum)*

Lavender *(Lavandula* species*)*

Lemon balm *(Melissa officinalis)*

Lemon verbena *(Aloysia triphylla)*

Sage *(Salvia officinalis)*

Wild marjoram *(Origanum vulgare)*

Decorative herbs

Alchemilla *(Alchemilla mollis)*

Bergamot *(Monarda fistulosa)*

Borage *(Borago officinalis)*

Blue Hyssop *(Hyssopus officinalis)*

Cardoon *(Cynara cardunculus)*

Chives *(Allium schoenoprasum)*

Curry plant *(Helichrysum angustifolium)*

Dill *(Anethum graveolens)*

Cone flower *(Echinacea* species*)*

Fennel *(Foeniculum vulgare)*

Lavender *(Lavandula* species*)*

Rue *(Ruta graveolens)*

Sage *(Salvia officinalis)*

Yarrow *(Achillea millefolium)*

Growing tips

All herbs need well-drained soil. To improve the structure of the soil, add bulky organic material such as garden compost, well-rotted manure or leafmould in spring once you've cleared any weeds.

■ Spread a mulch, such as leafmould or bark, which are low in nutrients and suit herbs well. This helps to retain moisture, suppress weeds and improve the condition of the soil.

■ In summer, lightly cut back herbs after flowering and feed them with liquid comfrey to encourage a second flush of leaves.

■ In autumn, dig in well-rotted manure or garden compost around established plants, but take care not to touch their stems.

■ In winter, protect tender herbs with horticultural fleece during cold snaps.

■ Raised beds are a good idea if your soil is unsatisfactory, or you want to make a feature of your herbs. When making a raised bed on top of soil, add a good layer of rubble followed by gravel and then at least 4cm (1½in) of topsoil mixed with grit or bark (three parts topsoil to one part grit or bark). The retaining walls should be 30–75cm (12–30in) high and made from sturdy materials such as logs, sleepers or bricks.

■ Don't plant dill and fennel together, as they cross-pollinate.

■ Control the roots of mint by either growing the plant in a large pot sunk in the ground, or containing it in the soil with a "box" made of slabs or tiles.

HARVEST & STORE ORCHARD FRUITS

The secret of successful harvesting is to know when to pick particular fruit. Some crops are best picked before they turn ripe; others, such as stone fruits, should be tree-ripened if you want the best flavour. Trees that have been grown in optimum conditions produce the best crops for storage; immature crops, or those that have received too little water and nutrients or suffered from pest and disease damage, won't store well. There are a few simple golden rules to follow when harvesting and storing orchard fruits to help preserve them for several months.

■ Fruit should always be harvested when it reaches optimum maturity – when it is the best quality. If a fruit is very ripe, it will soon start to deteriorate if it's not eaten.

■ Pick hard fruits such as apples and pears when they are just under-ripe, as they will continue to ripen once they have been picked. Fruit growing on the sunniest side of the tree will ripen first.

■ Careful handling is essential, as fruit can be easily bruised. Orchard fruits should be harvested by twisting and lifting the fruit up, not by pulling straight down, and placing it gently – not dropping it – into your harvesting containers. Apples and pears should be picked by holding the fruit with the palm of the hand and avoiding finger pressure. Leave the stalks intact.

■ Only pick fruit (this also applies to soft fruit) on a dry day, as any moisture will encourage mould. If it has rained the night before, wait a day or two before harvesting.

Tips on storing apples

● The ideal temperature for storing apples is 2–5°C (36–41°F).

● Medium-sized apples will store better than very small or very large apples.

● Store apples that ripen at different times separately. Earlier cultivars will speed up the maturity of later ones if they are stored together.

● Early-season varieties do not store well, and are best eaten quickly after harvesting, or cooked into a purée and stored in the freezer.

● Crops from mid-season cultivars can last well for four to five weeks if stored in the right conditions.

● Late-season varieties, which ripen in late September, can be stored for up to eight months. These fruits won't develop their full flavour until they have been stored for some time.

Storing fruits

Select only the best fruits for storing; any fruit that is bruised, has broken skin or shows signs of pest or disease damage should not be stored. The storeroom must be frost-free, safe from pests, rain-proof and ideally at a constant temperature with air circulating freely so that the atmosphere doesn't get too dry or hot and humid. Different crops have different temperature and humidity requirements, but a suitable average temperature is 4–7°C/40–50°F. A cool, dark outdoor storeroom or cellar is ideal; a garden shed or garage may need extra insulation in severe weather; basements and unheated rooms are also suitable; and attics are best avoided due to fluctuations in temperature and humidity.

■ Discard any fruit with bruises, blemishes or skin punctures, which will soon cause the fruit to rot.

■ Store the fruits slightly apart from each other in a single layer on slatted shelves, fruit trays or in boxes in a cool, dark place. Apples benefit from being wrapped individually in newspaper, or wax paper for prolonged life.

■ Cover the shelves or boxes with fine chicken wire to prevent pests nibbling the fruit.

■ Check your stored crops regularly – preferably weekly – and remove any fruits that are turning mouldy.

■ Pears are at their best for a short time only. Inspect them frequently, and bring them into a warm room when they are nearly ripe to finish off the process.

Storing citrus fruits

Lemons and other citrus fruits can be wrapped and stored much like apples, or you can keep them in boxes of sand. Put layers of unblemished fruits into wooden crates or paper-lined boxes and cover each layer with dry sand. The fruit should keep for up to two months in this way.

KEEP A MILKING COW

If you have the room and the commitment, a cow is a great addition to a smallholding. In return for grass, supplementary food in winter and good care, she will provide you with milk, cheese and butter.

Cows are hardy animals that can give a good return on your investment by providing many useful and saleable products, but they do require a high level of commitment. If you want to keep a cow for a near-constant supply of milk, then you will need to milk her twice a day, every day, and get involved in calving – a cow cannot produce her milk without newborn calves. So be prepared for the time involved: either you or someone else will always need to do the milking.

Signs of good health in a cow

- A shiny coat, with a gleam or "bloom" in the hairs.
- Bright eyes.
- A moist muzzle, and a clean (not runny) nose.
- Sweet breath.
- Soft, pliable udders free from lumps.

A cow's milk supply depends on how well she is fed and kept, and her general health.

Choose your cow

The main breeds of cow that will interest a smallholder are those that produce good quantities of high-quality milk, as well as good beef calves. The best approach is to purchase a three- to four-year-old "in-calf" (pregnant) cow that has already calved. She should also have been tested for tuberculosis. Your cow should have a useful, productive life of about 12 years.

Holstein Fresian
Large black and white cow. The breed is most commonly used in large-scale farming, as it is an excellent provider of milk. Because of its temperament and size, it needs skilful handling.

Jersey or Guernsey
These breeds provide very rich, good quality milk and have the advantage of being attractive, adaptable and docile animals. They are suited to a wide range of climates. Easily handled and milked.

Red Poll
An old breed, the Red Poll is a useful animal for milk and meat. It is very hardy and thrives outside. Naturally hornless. Easy to handle and a good feeder.

Caring for your cow

A cow is naturally a grazing animal, so she should be kept outdoors except in times of extreme weather – very cold and wet, or very hot. The precise conditions your cow will be able to withstand will depend on the breed, as some breeds are hardier than others, but a shed is a basic requirement. It must have straw bedding and be cleaned out daily when in use. All gates, fencing and hedges to your paddock must be strong. If you have a cow and a calf, you will need a good grazing meadow of at least two hectares (five acres) and access to water. If your cow has been transported by road to her new home, she will be stressed after her journey, so give her lots to drink and a good feed.

Feeding through the year

Grass is the best food for cows, and rich pasture results in rich milk. Your cow will get what she needs nutritionally from the grass during the summer, but in winter she will need supplementary feed in the form of roughage – straw or hay – and cereals for protein and carbohydrates, together with other foodstuffs such as kale or mangels (type of beet grown for livestock).

You will also need to provide what is called a "maintenance ration" for your cow – that is, what she needs for her own purposes, as well as a "production ration", which will help her to provide enough milk for your needs. It is best to ask your local smallholding or farming groups for advice on the recommended quantities of feed for your particular breed and climate, but as a guide you should provide 5.5–9 kilograms (12–20lb) of hay as a maintenance ration

Basic equipment

 Winter feed
Cows will nibble at grass in winter, but its nutritional value is very low at this time, so they need to eat hay, cereal feed such as rolled oats or barley, and root vegetables such as mangels.

 Salt lick
Mineral deficiencies can be fatal. Provide a block of salt and let your cow judge when and whether she needs it.

 Hay
Hay provides the required roughage in your cow's diet during the winter. It's worth making your own hay during the summer months.

4 Calf creep feeder
A durable creep feeder allows easy access to additional feed for small to medium-sized calves while they are still suckling the cow.

 Pasture
Your cow will need good summer pasture from spring to autumn if she is to provide you with a good supply of high-quality milk.

 Straw for bedding
During the winter, when your cow spends more time in her shed, she should have enough straw for deep bedding and to keep out draughts.

 Fencing
Spend a few moments every day checking that the fences enclosing your pasture are secure.

You should also ensure that you know a good vet, who is experienced in dealing with livestock, in case your cow contracts illness and diseases such as worms, mastitis, pneumonia, scours and New Forest Eye.

Milking a cow

Milk your cow every 12 hours, every day. Ask an experienced farmhand to show you how.

You can milk a cow outside, but it is better to milk her somewhere dry and clean, such as an area in a shed that can be thoroughly washed down. Use a sterilized stainless-steel bucket to collect the milk.

Distract your cow with a bucket of feed while you milk her – there's no real need to tie her up. Milking should be a predictable experience for the cow, as it will help to reassure and calm her. Sit on a stool at a right angle to the animal, always on the same side, and lean your head against her. This will be soothing for her, and you can feel if she's about to kick.

Use warm water to carefully clean the cow's udder. Take hold of the teat firmly, sealing the top with your thumb and index finger. Squeeze firmly downwards, closing your upper fingers first, to force the milk out. Let the teat go, allowing it to refill with milk. Then repeat the process. Be firm and confident as you milk, or the cow will detect hesitancy.

during the winter. It's a good idea to supplement the hay and balance your cow's diet by substituting half of the hay with other foods such as kale, mangels or cabbages in the appropriate quantities. This also helps to extend your supplies of precious and expensive hay. Again, experienced farmers will be able to advise you on how much to feed your cow. It's also a good idea to supplement your cow's diet with vitamins and minerals such as magnesium and calcium.

Cows drink prodigious amounts of water – up to 90 litres (20 gallons) each day – so make sure that you provide plenty of it. You should also provide what is called a "salt lick" – a block of salt in a bucket for your cow to taste as and when she sees fit.

Breeding

The time will come when your cow will need to produce a calf if you want her to keep producing milk. If she has already given birth, she should be "dried off" (when milking stops) 50 days before calving again. You can either introduce your cow to a bull, or have her artificially inseminated by a technician. You should be able to locate the services of a bull through local farming contacts, but it's worth bearing in mind that the size of the bull should match the size of your cow so that she doesn't struggle to carry the resulting calf.

Your cow can be inseminated when she is "in season", or ready to mate. She can indicate this by making loud noises and sometimes, but not always, discharging a mucus. Also, if she is kept with other cows, they will mount her when she is on heat. Being in season will happen at intervals, so if you choose a time in July, for example, to mate your cow, the calf will then be born in April when the grass is growing most strongly. The calf will be born nine months and seven days after your cow has been inseminated.

Feed your cow extra rations of cereal during the last eight weeks of her pregnancy: increase her feed gradually by 1 kilogram (2lb) of oats per day, up to 3.5 kilograms (8lb) per day until she gives birth.

If the weather is warm and her field is sheltered, your cow will prefer to calve in the open rather than in an unfamiliar barn. Her udder will fill and the muscles in her hind quarters will slacken noticeably, warning you that the birth is imminent. The calf should be born with its two front feet pointing forwards, with its head in between them. If you see that the calf is emerging in any other posture, you will need the help of a vet. If the newborn calf is able to cough and breathe, then just leave it to its mother, who will lick her calf with her rough tongue to clean it. She will also provide colostrum, a thick, yellow kind of milk, for the first few days after the calf's birth. After a day or so, when the calf is strong enough, disinfect its umbilical cord with iodine.

Weaning a calf

As you are keeping a cow for her milk, you may not want to wait for the calf to wean itself in 12 weeks' time, so you can force the issue by taking the calf away from its mother – gradually, at first, for a few hours at a time – when it is a week old. Check that the calf can drink diluted milk from a bucket, then lead it a few steps away from its mother where the animals can still see each other. Feed the calf hay as soon as it can eat, and by the autumn it can be turned into beef or kept for future milking, depending on its gender.

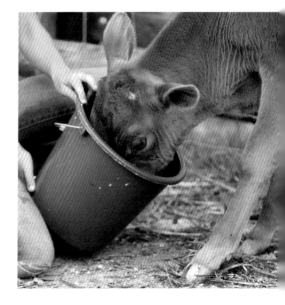

MAKE FRESHLY CHURNED BUTTER

Churning butter used to be a laborious and time-consuming process, but now that we have food processors to do all the hard work in a matter of moments, fresh, deliciously creamy butter is a quick and easy option.

Use fresh double cream, ideally at room temperature (about 15°C/60°F), for a sweet cream butter. If you want a more subtle continental flavour, culture the cream first before churning: add two tablespoons of crème fraîche, natural yoghurt or sour cream to 500ml (17fl oz) of fresh double cream. Leave the cream for 24 hours at a warm room temperature (about 24°C/75°F) and then cool it back down to 15°C (60°F) to make the butter. A digital food thermometer is a useful way of enabling you to control the temperature correctly without having to rely on guesswork.

- To make about 300g (10oz) of butter, measure 500ml (17fl oz) of fresh pouring double cream. The cream should be at room temperature.
- Fit the normal chopping blade to a food processor or a mixer and whip the cream – it will turn quickly from frothy to thick cream. The cream will stiffen further before separating into thick pale butterfat and buttermilk.
- Drain off the buttermilk (you can reserve it for making soda bread, or to drink).
- The remaining butterfat should be fluffy and ready to use as butter.

The butter will keep for longer if it's washed and worked at this point, which is an equally simple process: to wash it, add a cupful of iced water to the butterfat in the processor bowl and whizz the contents briefly. Pour off the milky water and repeat the process several times until the water remains clear after being whizzed with the butterfat. Then decant the butter into a bowl and use a potato masher or a couple of forks to press out the last of the liquid. If you wish, salt the butter to your taste and then roll it into a ball or a pat, or press it into ramekin dishes, and chill in the fridge. The butter should keep for a week or more.

MAKE ORGANIC DRINKS

It's always more pleasurable and satisfying to eat or drink something that you've grown or made yourself. Home-made drinks are a delicious way of enjoying a plentiful crop of fruits, or making something special and a little different for yourself or for guests. Bottled drinks that keep also make great gifts. Use seasonal produce to get the best quality and flavours.

Damson wine

Damson wine is one of the easiest and most successful of home-made wines to make. You will need some home brewing equipment:

A large plastic bucket

A one-gallon glass demi-john for the fermentation, plus an airlock to prevent air from entering the vessel while permitting the carbon dioxide gas produced by alcohol fermentation to escape.

A siphoning tube made of flexible plastic tubing attached to a few feet of hard plastic tubing. The hard tube goes into the demi-john to a point just above the sediment, and a quick suck on the soft end starts the movement of the clear liquid out of the demi-john.

Ingredients

1.4kg (3lb) ripe damsons, washed
6 pints water, plus ½ pint water
1 packet commercial wine yeast
1.4kg (3lb) unrefined organic sugar

Method

■ Put the damsons in a large, stainless steel pan, cover with the water and bring to the boil.
■ Allow to cool, then tip into a large bucket, cover with a cloth and leave overnight.

■ The following day, remove a little of the damson liquid, dissolve the yeast in it and leave for a few minutes until it appears bubbly. Then add it to the damsons, stir well with a wooden spoon and cover. Allow to ferment for three days, stirring well three times a day.

■ Gently dissolve the sugar in about ½ pint of water until it forms a clear syrup. Allow to cool, then stir into the damson mixture. Ferment for five days, stirring often.

■ Once the vigorous fermentation stops, strain the mixture and transfer it to a demi-john. Fit with an airlock and store at room temperature for about three months.

■ When the fermentation stops, remove the airlock and syphon into bottles, cork and leave for six months before drinking.

Variation
Elderberry wine
Use 1.4kg (3lb) of elderberries instead of damsons and follow the same method.

Spiced sloe gin

Ingredients

900g (2lb) sloes

25g (1oz) honey

Zest of 1 orange

Zest of 1 lemon

2.5cm (1in) cube fresh root ginger, thinly sliced

1 cinnamon stick

6 cloves

1 bottle of gin

Method

■ Lightly crush the sloes with the end of a wooden rolling pin.

■ Place in a wide-mouthed bottle and add the honey, orange and lemon zest, ginger, cinnamon stick and cloves.

■ Fill to the top with gin. Cork and leave in the larder for between 6–12 months.

Served with sparkling water, sloe gin makes a refreshing drink. Served neat, it makes a good aperitif or after-dinner drink.

Mint lemonade

Ingredients

110g (4oz) fresh mint leaves

Juice of 3 lemons

110g (4oz) sugar

700ml (1½ pints) water

Method

■ Blend the mint leaves, lemon juice and sugar together in a processor, then add the water.

■ Pour into a jug and chill well before serving.

Irish coffee

Ingredients

44ml (1½fl oz) Irish whisky

1 teaspoon brown sugar

180ml (6fl oz) strong filter coffee

Double cream to taste

Method

■ Combine whisky, sugar and coffee together in a mug or a glass. Stir well.

■ Place the tip of a dessert spoon at an angle into the coffee. Pour the cream over the back of the spoon so it floats on the coffee, and serve.

Apple cider lambswool

Ingredients

4 bramley apples, peeled and cored

1.2 litres (2 pints) cider

125g (4oz) fresh orange juice

8 whole allspice berries

2.5cm (1in) cube fresh root ginger, sliced

½ teaspoon nutmeg, freshly grated

125ml (4fl oz) brandy

Method

■ Roast the apples in a moderate oven until soft and pulpy.

■ Heat the remaining ingredients in a stainless steel pan (do not boil). Allow the spices to infuse for ten minutes, then scoop them out.

■ Stir in the apple pulp and serve.

Mulled wine

Ingredients

4 cloves

½ cinnamon stick

A few slices of fresh root ginger

Finely pared peel of 1 lemon

Finely pared peel of 1 orange

1 bottle red wine

1 tablespoon honey

A splash of brandy (optional)

Method

■ Put the spices, peel and wine in a pan. Heat to just below boiling point. Turn off the heat.

■ Leave to infuse for 1 hour. Then add the honey and brandy, gently reheat and serve.

KEEP A FLOCK OF DUCKS

Ducks are easy and versatile birds to keep, and although they can be noisy they also have an easy-going, cheerful demeanour. Depending on the breed, they can be a good source of meat, or produce up to 300 eggs each a year.

One of the attractions of keeping ducks is that they don't need elaborate housing – a simple duck house in your garden (or with a large run attached) will suit them well, as long as they have access to plenty of water. They will quickly rid your garden of slugs and snails, their droppings provide a good source of fertilizer and their used bedding can be added to other garden waste to produce organic compost. Ducks are gregarious birds and respond well to human conversation, becoming calmer and tamer as they get to know your voice.

Getting started

Ducks have few requirements, but it's important that they are happy and contented in their environment, and not overcrowded. You'll need a sufficiently large, securely enclosed area of grass (12.5sq m/15sq yds per bird) to allow for a variety of foraging material, and with lots of shady areas, as ducks don't like bright sunlight. Keep the birds away from ornamental gardens and vegetable plots, as they may destroy them. Ideally, your ducks should have clean running water to swim in – or, at the very least, enough clean water for them to immerse their heads and dabble. Dry, clean, predator- and draught-proof housing is also essential, as ducks need somewhere secure to roost overnight to protect them from vermin and foxes. They are sensitive creatures and don't like change, so try to keep their environment constant. They'll be upset by an object lying around, such as a spade, for example, and will try to avoid it, leading to stress.

Choose your ducks

There isn't a great choice of dual-purpose duck breeds that provide both eggs and meat, so you may decide to keep ducks either for the table or to lay eggs. Four to six ducks and a male, or drake, will be enough to establish a flock for meat, while four or five ducks should provide you with a good supply of eggs (you won't need a drake).

Saxony
This large, dual-purpose breed can lay reasonably well (about 150 eggs a year). A pretty, practical bird to keep, although the females can be noisy.

Indian Runner
A hardy duck, with an unusual upright stance. An excellent egg producer (about 300 eggs per year). Good natured, and average in terms of noise level.

Signs of good health in a duck

- Dry nostrils.
- Bright eyes with no soreness.
- Clean, shiny feathers.
- Good weight and musculature for age.
- Clean vent (rear end) feathers with no smell.
- Straight toes and undamaged webs.
- Alert and active with no sign of lameness.

Ducks are less prone to infections than chickens. Most ailments are caused by poor husbandry, such as lack of water, overcrowding or wet bedding. Stay aware of any news on avian flu and contact Defra for advice.

Muscovy
Generally a gentle breed, and the quietest. The females make good mothers. Suitable for the table.

Khaki Campbell
A prolific egg layer: the best strains are capable of laying well over 300 eggs per year. A practical, reasonably quiet duck.

Rouen Clair
A large, docile, dual-purpose breed: a reasonable egg layer, and its meat is tasty. A relatively quiet bird.

Once you have decided on a suitable breed, contact your local organic poultry club to get more advice, and look through smallholder magazines or go to waterfowl shows to find a suitable breeder. Always visit a breeder before buying any ducks.

Your ducks need to be taught where home is after you've bought them: to help them settle, keep new stock in a duck house with an outside run for a few days with plenty of clean straw, food and fresh water. Then let the ducks out at the start of each day to roam freely until dusk, when they should be shut up again. Most domestic ducks don't fly, but you can stop a bird from flying by clipping the flight feather short on one wing.

Feeding your ducks

Ducks need fresh water and grass, grain and grit to feed on. Grit is essential to help them digest their food, and if it's not available in your garden, supply it in a shallow box or a flower pot, in a dry place. Ducks will forage for their own food and add worms, insects, slugs and snails to their normal grass and plant diet. If possible, move the duck house to a new area of grass every so often to reduce the risk of disease and the destruction of your lawn. You need only supplement the ducks' own foraging with a basic organic grain ration, provided first thing in the morning and at dusk in a feeder trough in the duck house. However, ducks that are laying or being fattened up for meat will need additional feeding with organic mixed corn and protein.

Duck eggs

Ducks will lay eggs from midwinter to midsummer, and a healthy duck will remain productive for around three years. To encourage good egg production, the darkest

end of the duck house should have boards to provide an attractive nesting area. Keep the area comfortable with a layer of straw, and add some large china eggs to encourage your ducks to start laying their own. Collect the eggs regularly to discourage vermin attacks, prevent ducks becoming broody and to avoid damaged eggs. The shells of duck eggs are more porous than those of hens, so hygiene is vital: wipe the shells immediately with a damp cloth. The eggs have a short shelf-life of one week and are best eaten fresh.

A duck keepers kit

❶ Duck house
The house can be simple, but must be kept dry and clean (removable sides make this easy). Protect from damp and rot with an organic wood preservative. Each bird needs 60 sq cm (2 sq ft) of roosting space. Clean the duck house at least once a week.

❷ Hose
Essential for keeping the floor of the duck house thoroughly clean.

❸ Feeding hopper

❹ Fresh water
Ducks need a constant supply of fresh drinking water.

❺ Water to bathe in
A stream or clean pond is ideal, but a large, deep water trough, or rigid plastic sandpit, with a ramp is fine, if it's cleaned regularly.

❻ Feed
Organic mixed corn and protein can be bought in pellet form, or make your own mash from ground grains (oats, maize and barley) and protein.

❼ Fresh straw
Use straw, hay or newspaper to keep the floor of the duck house dry.

USE UP A GLUT OF TOMATOES

Tomatoes are fully ripened and perfect for picking once they have turned a lovely rich red colour. Home-grown tomatoes are full of delicious flavour and goodness that's too good to waste, so if you have a large crop ripening at the same time, it's worth making soup or preserves that you can freeze or store for later in the year.

Tomato & fennel soup

(serves 4)

Ingredients

1 red onion, diced

1 tablespoon olive oil

4 cloves garlic, chopped

1 teaspoon fennel seed, ground

2 fennel bulbs, coarse outer leaves removed and sliced very thinly

900g (2lb) ripe tomatoes, quartered and deseeded

1.2 litres (2 pints) vegetable stock

1 teaspoon tomato purée

Salt and pepper

Method

■ Cook the onion in the olive oil in a large thick-based stainless steel pot until soft. Add the garlic and fennel seed. Cook for two minutes.

■ Add the sliced fennel bulbs, tomatoes and the stock, bring to the boil and simmer gently for 20 minutes.

■ Remove from the heat and stir in the tomato purée. Season with salt and pepper to taste and blend in a food processor. Leave to cool.

■ Decant into sealable containers and freeze.

Oven-dried tomatoes

The flavour of tomatoes is intensified by slowly roasting them in an oven. Cherry tomatoes are the easiest to use (yellow and red varieties work equally well), and cherry plum tomatoes are particularly good. It's worth preparing as many tomatoes as possible at a time, and use as much garlic and herbs as you like.

- Preheat the oven to 145°C/200°F/Gas 2.
- Lightly oil a baking tray with olive oil.

- Cut a quantity of tomatoes in half and place them skin side down on a baking tray.
- Finely slice some cloves of garlic and place them on top of the tomatoes. Scatter over finely chopped thyme or rosemary, a little sea salt and a scant amount of sugar. Put the tray in the oven.
- Bake for about three hours. Check regularly that the tomatoes don't become over-dried.
- Store in a sealed container in the fridge – they will keep for about a week.

Tomato & chilli chutney

Ingredients

1kg (2lb 4oz) ripe tomatoes

500g (1lb) onions, chopped

2 chillies, chopped

6 cloves garlic, chopped

500g (1lb) unrefined sugar

500ml (17fl oz) white wine vinegar

500ml (17fl oz) water

2 bay leaves

Salt and pepper

Method

■ Cut the tomatoes in half and scrape out the seeds and juice from the middle. Reserve the seeds and juice.

■ In a heavy-based saucepan, gently cook the onions, chilli and garlic in the oil until soft. Then add the tomato seeds and juice, along with the sugar, vinegar, water and bay leaves.

■ Bring to the boil and simmer gently for about an hour or until reduced by half.

■ Roughly chop the tomato halves, season with salt and pepper and add them to the pan.

■ Boil the chutney for a further 10 minutes, then remove the pan from the heat.

■ Sterilize some jars by washing them well and placing them in a moderate oven for five minutes. Then fill them with the chutney, secure the lids firmly and store in a cool, dry place.

KEEP A GOAT OR TWO

Goats are relatively hardy animals, well-suited to many climates and ideal for a smallholding. They can be kept for their good supplies of nutritious milk or reared for their low-fat meat. They are affectionate creatures but, if given the slightest opportunity, they can create havoc in a garden.

Many people keep goats for their milk; goat's milk and cheese are becoming popular alternatives to traditional dairy foods made with cow's milk, which some people have an intolerance to. In addition to milk and possibly meat, goats' manure makes good organic fertilizer and the hair of some breeds can be turned into soft mohair, angora or cashmere.

Goats are very sociable animals and love company, so you should plan to keep more than one unless you have other animals to live with it. Goats are related to sheep but, unlike their relatives, they are not natural "lawn mowers" when it comes to grazing. They are choosy and can be obstinate, and may reject the finest meadow grass for a piece of paper or a weed that's just out of reach. Goats can also stand on their hind legs to reach leaves they particularly like to eat on bushes and small trees, and any plant can be a potential meal – including your flowers and vegetables. So you'll need to outwit your goats and keep them fenced in or tethered. They also require a dry shed to shelter from bad weather, plus fresh water and some additional feed.

Goat's milk

A goat needs to be pregnant to produce milk, and after the birth of kids, it can give milk for almost a year. If the goat is not mated again, it can be milked for up to two years without interruption. Milk production increases with age: a mature nanny goat can give 3.5 litres (7 pints) of milk per day compared to a young nanny goat, which may give half this amount. Female goats come into season during their first autumn; most have two kids, and give birth without much difficulty. You can then decide whether to keep or sell the kids.

Choose your goats

There are a range of breeds that a smallholder can consider. Choose your breed according to whether you want goats for their milk or meat. The productive life of a goat is about six years. Male goats reach sexual maturity at three months, when they can be used for meat.

Toggenburg
The smallest and most compact of the dairy breeds, originally from Switzerland. It can give good supplies of milk, and is extremely affectionate.

Anglo-Nubian
A short-coated variety with long drooping ears and a distinctive "Roman" nose. Produces high yields of rich milk, which is good for making cheese and yoghurt.

If you want to keep goats for milk production, you must be prepared to milk them twice a day, every day, and give them regular attention. Neglect or irregularities in milking can quickly lead to health problems in milk goats. A milking goat should be fed and housed at night, and turned out to graze in between milking.

Keep your goats healthy

Goats need a secure area where they have some freedom and stimulation – preferably in the form of a scrambling area – plus a dry, draught-proof shelter, a balanced diet and plenty of water. Goats are naturally healthy animals, and although they can be susceptible to some unpleasant conditions, good husbandry will help to prevent this.

Good levels of hygiene, clean food and water and appropriate living conditions are the best protection against illness. As with any animal, keep a watchful eye on a goat to identify any change in behaviour or appearance. Call your vet if you spot any signs of injury, if the animal's eyes become dull, if it isn't eating or drinking normally, or if it stops producing milk.

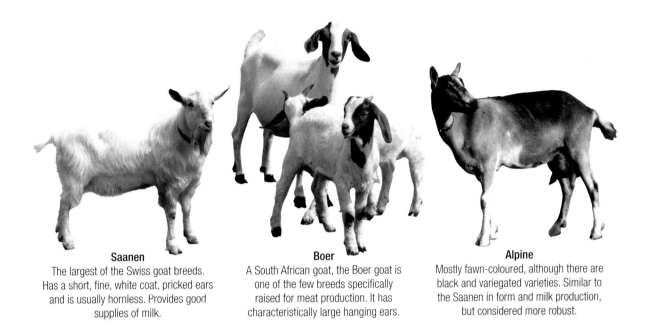

Saanen
The largest of the Swiss goat breeds. Has a short, fine, white coat, pricked ears and is usually hornless. Provides good supplies of milk.

Boer
A South African goat, the Boer goat is one of the few breeds specifically raised for meat production. It has characteristically large hanging ears.

Alpine
Mostly fawn-coloured, although there are black and variegated varieties. Similar to the Saanen in form and milk production, but considered more robust.

It's essential to look after your goats' feet. The hoofs of goats living in their original mountain habitats are constantly worn down by the rough rocks, but on a domestic smallholding they will need be trimmed on a regular basis and kept as dry as possible to prevent foot rot. Trim the hoofs flat so that the goat can stand comfortably. If you are not able to trim them yourself with a sharp knife or foot trimmers, ask your vet to do it.

Like sheep, goats are susceptible to worms and coccidiosis. You can reduce the incidence of these infections by employing a "clean grazing" strategy, which requires areas used for grazing by goats in the spring to have been kept free from all animals for at least one year. Alternatively, you should ask your vet to worm your goats regularly. Remember that you shouldn't consume milk from wormed goats for at least seven days after worming. You should also regularly inspect your goats for lice, which will make them very uncomfortable and require treatment.

A goat keepers kit

1 **Goat house**
Each goat requires a minimum of 2sq m (6sq ft) of space inside a goat house or shed, which can also be used for milking. The shed should be tall enough for the goats to stand up on their hind legs with their necks outstretched. The shed should also be draught-proof.

2 **Strong fencing**
Goats will escape, given the opportunity, so they need to be tethered securely or confined behind strong, high fencing.

3 **Mineral block**
Fix a mineral lick to the wall of the goat house so that your goats get enough minerals in their diet.

4 **Grazing area**
Rough scrubland, hedges and bushes all provide good grazing for goats. If possible, give them plenty of space to graze and roam around.

5 **Fresh water**
Goats need fresh supplies of water. Firmly securing a bucket of water down prevents a goat from kicking it over.

6 **Secure areas**
A bar above a stable-type shed door will stop a goat jumping out.

7 **Feed**
As well as grass, goats need rations of grain and hay, which must be available at all times. Secure the hay racks with bars to stop goats pulling out too much hay at once. Milking goats need extra feed of concentrates, such as flaked maize, rolled oats or crushed beans.

Basic equipment

Unlike sheep and cattle, which can stay out in all weathers, goats need a dry shed where they can shelter from the wet and cold. A wooden or concrete floor is best, covered with comfortable bedding. Ideally, the house should have a concrete yard attached so that the goats have some freedom outside in bad weather.

Good strong fences are essential; normal barbed wire or netting fences are not adequate. To restrain goats, use either chain-link fences (at least 1.2m/4ft high) topped by barbed wire, or three to four strands of electric fence (at least 1m/3ft 6in high).

If you tether a goat, keep a constant eye on her: provide her with water, protect her from other animals such as dogs, and move her out of the sun or rain.

Feeding

Goats will forage for about half of their diet and eat shrubs, gorse and brambles. They will also eat any vegetable scraps you can provide. While they are being milked, they also need about 1–2 kilograms (2–4lb) of a concentrate ration, and 1–2 kilograms (2–4lb) of hay and roots per day during the winter months. Kid goats need about 1.2 litres (2 pints) of milk for the first two to three months, before being weaned onto a diet of hay and concentrate. The feed should be placed in troughs at goat head-height in the goat house so that the goats can reach it, but not foul it. A ready supply of clean drinking water is also essential.

MAKE A SIMPLE GOAT'S CHEESE

The fresh, tangy flavour of goat's cheese is a wonderful addition to a cheese board. It's much easier to make soft cheese than it is to make hard cheese, and different herbs can be added to enhance the flavour.

The principle of making milk into cheese is simple: the milk is soured with a bacterial culture, then rennet (an enzyme from the stomach of cows) is added, which causes curds to form – the basic ingredient of cheese. The cheese is separated from the whey, then salted and dried.

- Warm 4.5 litres (8 pints) of fresh goat's milk in a large pan to 32°C (90°F).
- Stir in the starter, a bacterial culture that creates acidity. Either buy the starter or make it: the method consists of leaving some unpasteurized milk (approx 125ml/4fl oz) to turn sour.

■ Leave to stand for 45 minutes, then add rennet (according to the instructions on the packet). The curds may take 12 hours to coagulate fully. When the curds split easily if you push your finger through them, they are ready.

■ Strain the curds through cheesecloth (which should be scalded to prevent the cheese from going bad) to drain off the whey. Tie the corners of the cloth together and hang the curds to drain overnight.

■ Add a little salt to taste. Use the fresh curds as cheese, or put the curds into moulds lined with cheesecloth and leave weights on top. More whey will drain out, so the cheeses will become firmer.

■ If you wish, roll the shaped cheeses in finely chopped fresh herbs of your choice, or nuts, and store in the fridge.

PLANT A VINE

With its thick woody stem and large leaves that turn burnished shades in autumn, a grapevine (*Vitis vinifera*) is a wonderful, vigorous climber to grow in a garden. It will scramble over pergolas to create shady areas, or decorate walls or fences.

If you plant a vine in a sunny corner in well-drained soil and leave it to its own devices, it will produce some bunches of edible grapes, although eventually the leaves will take over and there'll be less fruit. If you're prepared to take a bit of time choosing the right variety and train it and prune it every year, then you should be rewarded with the first of countless bunches of fully flavoured grapes for the table, for juice or for winemaking just three years after planting. A well-tended vine can produce top-quality grapes for 40 years or more.

Growing grapes organically will guarantee that they have not been sprayed with chemicals, as most supermarket ones are, and picking them when fully ripe will give you the sweetest of fruits. Vines are not fussy plants, and once they establish their root systems they get the moisture and nutrients they need from deep in the soil. They won't survive in waterlogged soil, however, or produce good fruit in nitrogen-rich soil. While the bunches of fruit hang on the stems, they won't ripen fully unless the temperature is at least 10°C (50°F).

Most vines prefer:

■ **Well-drained soil** free from perennial weeds, with a pH (this measures its acidity) of 6.3–6.8. Ideally, the soil should be prepared before planting by digging in garden compost, with added grit on heavy soils. Some varieties will not grow well in alkaline soils.

■ **A sunny site** less than 200m (650ft) above sea level: in temperate climates, plant against a wall or fence that faces south, south east or south west, with the planting hole at least 15cm (6in) from the base. Vines need dry, warm weather at flowering time to set fruit.

■ **Regular watering** when newly planted, to encourage the roots to grow down and out into the soil.

■ **Mulching** with garden compost in spring.

Varieties to grow outdoors

Grapes need plenty of warmth to ripen fully outdoors. In cooler areas, it's best to grow early ripening dessert varieties – very late ripening ones, such as Black Hamburg, need the extra warmth and protection of a greenhouse. Grapes are susceptible to various fungal diseases so it is worth choosing ones that have the greatest resistance to disease.

Dessert grapes/white wines

1. Siegerrebe
2. Himrod
3. Madeleine Angevine
4. Seibel

Dessert grapes/red wines

5. Regent
6. Leon Millot
7. Triomphe d'Alsace
8. Boskoop Glory

Buying & planting a vine

Vines for sale in specialist nurseries are usually grafted onto phylloxera-resistant rootstock (phylloxera is a pest that attacks the roots of vines. In the nineteenth century, it almost wiped out all the vines in Europe). It's a good idea to choose your plants from a specialist grower and get advice on the best varieties and how to train and prune them. Dessert grapes are larger than wine grapes and rarely make good wine. Some wine grapes, however, are sweet enough to eat.

Vines climb by tendrils and need support. They can be grown free-standing on wires supported by sturdy posts and trained horizontally and vertically against the wires. Or they can be grown up posts and trained into heart or goblet shapes, over a wheel or up and over a pergola. A vine against a wall should be trained up a cane and onto heavy-duty galvanized wires with a 4cm (1½in) gap behind them.

How vines are trained depends on the grape variety and on factors such as doors or walls in a wall. Whatever the method, a vine should be cut back hard on planting, and again at the end of the first season. The purpose of pruning, which should be done every winter (and with some lighter pruning and thinning in summer) encourages the plant to produce regular crops of good-sized grapes. For dessert grapes, special scissors with long thin blades are useful for snipping off some of the smaller bunches to allow larger bunches more space and light.

Picking ripe grapes

Grapes start to ripen once they change from green. It's best to leave them on the vine until the sugar content increases fully – this can take anything from a few weeks to a couple of months, depending on the variety. The best way to test their ripeness is to taste them. Traditionally grapes are cut with enough stalk to make a "T" shape so that they can be carried without being touched. Handling the grapes damages the "bloom" – the waxy coating on the skins – which helps to protect the fruits and deflects rainwater while they grow.

FEED BENEFICIAL WILDLIFE IN WINTER

Many of the insects and other small creatures that live in gardens hibernate through the cold winter months, so they need safe, weatherproof places to hide in. They also need plenty of food in autumn in order to fatten up before becoming inactive. Other wildlife, such as birds and larger mammals, that keep going through winter need regular supplies of food and drinking water. You can help all the wildlife in your garden to survive for another season by being aware of what they need and ensuring that you provide it.

Plan ahead

■ **Leave some part of the garden undisturbed** where insects and other small creatures can take shelter. This can be an area of tussocky grass, a pile of leaves or decaying plants, or plant stems left standing through the winter months.

■ **Grow berrying and fruiting plants** in your garden or on your plot of land, including some native species such as hawthorn, blackthorn, rowan, crab apple, elder, ivy, pyracantha, cotoneaster, rugosa rose and bramble. These plants will provide a supply of food for birds and small mammals.

■ **Leave seed heads** of plants such as teasel, sunflowers and fennel standing so that seed eaters such as finches can help themselves. Seed heads can also provide winter quarters for some minibeasts.

■ **Make a pile of logs** or sticks in a quiet spot to provide a wintering site for a community of animals from woodlice, spiders and hoverflies to toads, frogs and slow-worms. If you bury the logs at the bottom of the pile in the soil, stag, rhinoceros and longhorn beetles may even take up residence in the decaying wood.

Extra help for birds

Putting out extra food on bird tables and in feeders during the winter months can be a lifesaver for many birds, especially in city gardens and when there is snow on the ground. The more feeders the better, and a variety of foods will attract different species.

Black sunflower seeds are one of the best all-round foods – use sunflower hearts if you don't want a scattering of husks under the feeder. Goldfinches will flock to eat nyjer seeds, while house sparrows, tits and greenfinches enjoy peanuts. Put the whole nuts in wire mesh feeders so that they can't be fed to young birds. Avoid salty food and stale bread, which can be harmful. Some birds, such as the song thrush, dunnock and wren, prefer to find their food on the ground. To feed these birds, make or buy a low table and cover it with a protective cage. Bird tables should be cleaned with a mild detergent from time to time to prevent infections spreading. You can also make balls of bird food to hang up (mix 400g/14oz of oats, nuts, seeds and dried fruit with 500g/18oz of melted lard and, when cool, roll into balls and thread pieces of string with a knot in the end through the centres with a needle). Fresh water for drinking and bathing is vital too. In freezing weather, keep a birdbath from icing over completely by floating a ball on the surface, or defrost it using hot water.

Nesting sites

From early spring onwards, birds need nesting sites. The trunks of mature trees, thick leafy climbers, hedges and holes in walls all provide natural sites. You can also offer extra nests by putting up boxes, either open-fronted for birds such as robins and wrens, or hole-fronted for tits, starlings, house sparrows, nuthatches and owls. It is easy and cheap to make your own nest using pieces of weatherproofed wood and galvanized screws and nails, or you can buy one of the huge range of ready-made ones. Put up nest boxes in autumn, and position them out of strong sunlight and driving rain, so that the birds have plenty of time to find them.

Food & shelter for hedgehogs

Hedgehogs need to fatten up in early autumn, so you can put out meat-based pet food, plus some dried cat food biscuits, to supplement their natural diet of beetles, worms and other invertebrates. Thick piles of dried leaves at the bottom of a hedge or dense climber, piles of branches and compost heaps will make good hibernating sites for hedgehogs, but you can also put out purpose-made wooden or willow hedgehog houses and fill them with straw. In mild winters, hedgehogs may not need to hibernate. If they don't take up residence, wood mice or voles might instead.

Insect homes

To encourage beneficial insects such as ladybirds, lacewings and bees to stay on your land, you can make overwintering homes for them. Cut up short lengths of cane or hollow plant stems, cram them into an open-fronted box or tube and hang the tube in a sheltered spot. There are also ready-made versions of these shelters available to buy. For solitary bees and wasps, drill holes of different sizes in pieces of dead wood. Position your bee and wasp homes in areas where the insects' activities will not disturb you while you are in the garden.

Did you know

● In Britain, 700 species of beetle live off decaying wood. More than half of these species are rare or threatened.

● Grass snakes sometimes use compost heaps as nesting sites. The warmth of the rotting vegetation provides ideal conditions for incubating their eggs.

● In response to the colder air temperatures of winter, a hedgehog's body temperature drops from around 35°C to 10°C or less while it is hibernating,

PLANT & SOW BY THE MOON

For organic gardeners, the key to growing healthy, strong plants is fertile soil that has good structure and supplies of nutrients. Some gardeners believe that the moon plays a vital role in plant growth and development too. They hold that the moon's gravitational pull, to which scientists attribute the rise and fall of the Earth's oceans, also affects the Earth's water table, causing increased amounts of moisture to move up into the topsoil. The period from a new moon to a full moon (the waxing moon), when increased moisture is available to seeds and plants, is the best time to sow and plant. The period from a full moon to the next new moon (the waning moon), when the moisture content is at its lowest and there's less sap rising in trees and shrubs, is the time to prune.

To benefit from these lunar influences, people who practise gardening by the moon draw up an annual calendar and tend their plants accordingly. Biodynamic gardeners and farmers, who follow the teachings of Austrian philosopher Rudolph Steiner, also use lunar calendars, but theirs are more complex, as they believe that plants are affected by wider planetary rhythms, and that crops are linked to one of the four traditional elements – earth, water, air and fire – depending on whether they are root, leaf, flower or seed crops. Each crop must be planted when the moon is in the sign of the zodiac associated with that element.

Biodynamic gardening methods involve keeping the soil full of vitality by adding compost and manure, and special therapeutic preparations made from plant, mineral and animal material. Crops grown this way, it is claimed, are more vigorous and taste better.

CREATE A POND FOR WILDLIFE

The pressure on land for agriculture, housing and commercial development has meant that many ponds and wetlands that native wildlife depend on are becoming polluted or have been drained. Garden ponds are important havens for these creatures, so a pond designed and made with wildlife in mind, and planted with the right plants, will soon be colonized by a host of creatures – from tiny water organisms and plankton to visiting birds and mammals.

Snails and small crustaceans will arrive on birds' feet or attached to plants; diving beetles, water fleas, water boatmen and pond skaters may soon be spotted scurrying through the water; insects such as dragonflies and damselflies will fly in and start to breed; and birds will fly down to drink and bathe. Later, frogs, toads and newts may take up residence, and mammals such as hedgehogs, foxes and badgers could become regular visitors.

Any container of fresh water will attract some wildlife, but a specially designed pond is one of the best ways of providing for a wide variety of creatures. Site the pond in a spot where plants have enough sunlight to grow.

Wildlife ponds can be different shapes, sizes and depths, but they all need:
- Clean water with low levels of nutrients.
- Shallow edges that shelve, to allow different plants to flourish and creatures to climb or crawl out of the pond easily.
- An area of pond that is 60cm (24in) deep so that creatures can survive hot summers and freezing winters.
- Plant cover that includes some native species to create shade and shelter – about two-thirds plants to one-third open water is ideal.

How to make a wildlife pond

● Decide on the size and shape of the pond and mark it out with a length of hose or sand. Site it away from large trees, as their roots may disturb or pierce the pond base, and fallen leaves lying on the water deplete it of oxygen as they decay. Dig the hole with gently sloping shelves around the sides.

● Remove any sharp stones, roots or debris. Line the base with a layer of sand or matting, then lay down the liner, leaving extra around the sides so that the edges can be buried under turf or other edging such as stone slabs or pebbles. Use a good-quality strong rubber or plastic liner that won't tear (buy the liner from a pond supplier). Alternatively, line the base with puddled clay.

● Fill the hole with water. The weight of the water will mould the liner to the shape of the pond. Hide the edges of the liner under grass or other edging. If using tap water, allow it to stand for 48 hours before planting or introducing wildlife. For a good balance of water wildlife, don't stock the pond with fish. Even small sticklebacks are voracious and will devour spawn and adult insects.

Planting in a pond

Pond life is adapted to native plants, so include a variety of these, as well as any exotics you might like. (Some non-native plants can be difficult to eradicate once they get established, and choke up ponds and rivers, so be careful what you plant.) Introduce rooted plants in mesh baskets and cover the soil or compost in the basket with gravel to prevent it washing away.

Free-floating submerged plants help to oxygenate the water and provide hiding places for deeper water creatures. Examples are curled pondweed *(Potamogeton crispus)*, water milfoil *(Myriophyllum spicatum)*, rigid hornwort *(Ceratophyllum demersum)* and water crowfoot *(Ranunculus aquatilis)*.

Floating plants rest their leaves on the surface of the water and help to provide shade and cover. Examples are yellow water lily *(Nuphar lutea)*, frogbit *(Hydrocharis morsus-ranae)*, broad-leaved pondweed *(Potamogeton natans)* and water soldier *(Stratiotes aloides)*.

Shallow water plants, many of which have attractive flowers, provide stems for emerging nymphs to climb up and roots where invertebrates can shelter. Examples are bogbean *(Menyanthes trifoliata)*, water forget-me-not *(Myosotis scorpioides)* and yellow flag iris *(Iris pseudacorus)*.

Pond-edge flowering plants provide nectar for butterflies, bees and other insects. Examples are marsh marigold *(Caltha palustris)*, ragged robin *(Lychnis flos-cuculi)* and meadowsweet *(Filipendula ulmaria)*.

Tips on pond care

- Skim off duckweed (*Lemna* species) when it gets too dense.

- Rake off or scoop out leaves from the surface of the water.

- In hot weather, top up the pond, ideally with rain water.

- In winter, pull and lift out any plants that are taking over and cut back any dead plants.

- In freezing weather float a ball on the pond to prevent the water totally icing over. Take the ball out to create an air hole for pond creatures.

- After removing blanketweed, leave it at the side of the pond for 24 hours to allow any small creatures in it to return to the water. Clear only a quarter of the weed at a time to allow wildlife to get used to changes in light and oxygen levels.

- Don't expect crystal-clear water. Green water means that it is full of algae, but the water soon turns a natural brownish colour once small water creatures start to feed on them. You can speed up this process by introducing some water fleas (Daphnia species) from an established pond. If this doesn't work, throw in a net of barley straw. For the correct amount, check with a specialist aquatic centre.

RAISE A COUPLE OF YOUNG PIGS

Pigs are intelligent and sensitive creatures, but they are also hardy, versatile animals that flourish well in a smallholding, eating up household food scraps, foraging for themselves and providing an efficient source of meat and fertilizer.

Originally descended from woodland foraging creatures, today's domestic pigs are one of the most productive of all livestock animals for converting feed to meat, as well as producing valuable manure for the smallholder. They can rotavate ground effectively or, if kept in orchards, they will control the weeds, fertilize the earth and eat up the windfalls.

In addition, pigs are friendly and sociable animals, and it's easy for you and your family to form bonds with them. Unfortunately, this may make parting with them difficult when the time comes to send them to the abattoir to be slaughtered. On the positive side, though, breeding your own pigs for meat provides a good source of delicious pork, bacon, sausages and brawn, and possibly some extra income. Pigs are ready to be slaughtered at 26 weeks old, but they need to be kept and fed for about ten months if they are to be used for bacon.

Where to start

It is a good idea to begin by visiting local agricultural shows and talking to pig farmers and other smallholders before you start looking for a reputable breeder. In this way, you can build up your knowledge before you buy any livestock. Smallholder magazines

Signs of good health in a pig

Don't go just on looks when choosing pigs, unless you are interested in buying pedigree animals. Instead, buy pigs with good, easy-going temperaments. Signs of good health include:

● A moist snout.

● Bright eyes – if the pig's ears cover its eyes, look underneath the ears to check the eyes.

● A shiny coat, with the hairs lying close to the body (a dull coat can be a sign of ill-health).

● A curly tail; a straight tail may indicate illness.

A lack of appetite, loss of energy, lameness, scouring or diarrhoea could indicate an infection or disease.

are also a good source of information on potential stock to buy. Before you do consider buying, check that you can provide your pigs with the right shelter, enough space and some earth to dig around in.

Always keep at least two pigs, as they love company. Perhaps the best, and cheapest, way to start is to buy young pigs, or "weaners", which are weaned from their mothers at around six to eight weeks old. Pigs at this age can be trained and handled more easily, and are easier to introduce to the food you'll feed them on. Older pigs are more fussy. Another option is to purchase a sow "in pig", meaning that she will soon give birth to a litter of piglets. Keeping a sow is essential if you intend to breed your own pigs as a source of meat and income.

Choose your pigs

The type of pig you buy depends on how you will want to use or sell the meat. Some pigs are ideal for dual-purpose use: in other words, they can be kept for both pork and bacon. The older and less developed the breed, the hardier it will be; such breeds are easy for a smallholder to keep. These are some of the most suitable breeds.

Large White
A popular modern breed, now used widely because of its productivity. Can get sunburned outside in warm climates.

Saddleback
A rare and distinctive-looking breed. Good mothering instincts. Dual-purpose (there is a slight discoloration of the meat).

Large Black
A rare, hardy breed that copes in cold temperatures. A good pasture feeder and breeder. Bred primarily for bacon.

Tamworth
A rare, very old breed with a golden-red coat. Ideal for outdoor rearing, it is hardy, athletic and a good rotavator. Dual-purpose.

Middle White
A rare, hardy breed that is alert and curious, but also docile. A consistently good breeder, and bred for its pork.

Gloucester Old Spot
A rare breed at home in a cold climate. It breeds and forages well and has a good temperament. Dual-purpose.

Hampshire
A hardy American breed similar to the Saddleback. A good breeder and forager. Easy to handle, despite its large size.

Berkshire
A rare breed with a black coat, white feet, a white face and white tail tip. Copes well in cold temperatures. Bred for pork.

Duroc
A hardy American breed originally bred for lard. A good breeder with a docile temperament. Bred for bacon.

Looking after your pigs

Pigs aren't demanding animals, but they do need regular attention and more space than you might assume. They need to be fed twice a day, must have warm, dry shelter and require sufficient earth and water to dig around and bathe in.

The best environment

For really healthy and happy pigs, you should allow them enough space to roam around and dig about in open ground. An area of around 300 square metres (360sq yds) is preferable for two pigs. The ground should be dry and not marshy, with good drainage. Avoid stony ground, as pigs have a tendency to hurt their feet on stones and rocks. Pigs don't need to feed on the best grass, and will eradicate weeds and help plough the soil. Ideally, if you can, allow them to forage in an orchard or in woodland, which will provide them with good food and plenty of interest.

Basic requirements

Pigs need soil and grass for the vitamins and minerals they contain, and they like to dig and forage for worms. They also need a pool of water, or water hole, to bathe in. A coating of mud helps to protect their skin from sunburn and keeps them cool in the sun. Top up their baths regularly with clean water in hot weather, or even hose them down on particularly hot days.

Pigs are intelligent animals and can get bored in a small space, so give them as large an area to live in as possible, secured with two lines of electric fencing (10cm/4in and 20cm/8in above the ground) or pig netting fixed to strong posts. Move your pigs to new ground when they have exhausted supplies of grass and grubs to reduce the chances of worms or other ailments.

Pigs also need warm, dry areas to shelter from harsh weather, to sleep in and to bear piglets. These need only be simple structures that can be easily moved, and you can buy them or make them yourself. Provide the pigs with a comfortable bed of clean straw regularly.

Feeding

As well as eating grass – particular favourites are couch grass and clover – and worms and nutrients in the soil, pigs need a supplement of pig nuts (a grain-based feed) and water to drink. You can also feed them wheat, barley, soya and fruit and vegetable scraps, although some vegetables, such as potatoes, should be cooked. Don't give them any feed containing animal meat. If you have any spare or waste whole or skimmed milk, however, pigs will love this added to their cereal. Feed your pigs twice a day at the same time; if you don't, they will notice and become irritable.

Settling your pigs

When you bring your pigs home, keep them in a small pen with a shelter, or a sty, for a few days. Give them lots of fresh water and feed them twice a day until they are used to the routine. Then let them out to graze.

A pig keeper's kit

1 Shelter or arc
A basic hut made from simple materials, such as iron or wood, will enable a pig to shelter from sun and rain and house any piglets she may have.

2 Hose
Use a hose to top up the pigs' water holes or wallowing area.

3 Fresh water
All pigs need a constant supply of clean, fresh water to drink, but sows in milk need even more. Fix the water trough securely to the ground and make sure that the piglets can reach over the rim to drink the water.

4 Household scraps
Pigs will happily eat household scraps (they should never be given meat).

5 Straw
Provide plenty of straw for the pig sty or shelter at least once a month.

6 Feed
The best feed for pigs is soaked barley meal and "middlings" or "sharps" – a fine wheat bran – and pig nuts.

4 DIRECTORY

DIRECTORY

Babies & Children

Clothes & bedding
Ecotopia www.ecotopia.co.uk
Gossypium www.gossypium.co.uk
Greenfibres www.greenfibres.com
House of Winkle www.houseofwinkle.co.uk
Hug www.hug.co.uk
Huggababy www.huggababy.co.uk
Organics for Kids www.organicsforkids.com
Tel 01865 311410
People Tree www.ptree.co.uk
Schmidt Natural Clothing www.naturalclothing.co.uk

Nappies
For information on nappy services:
National Association of Nappy Services
info@changenappy.co.uk Tel 0121 693 4949
The Real Nappy Association
www.realnappy.com.co.uk Tel 020 8299 4519

Other useful websites:
www.greenchoices.org
www.nappyfacts.co.uk
www.spiritofnature
www.thenappylady.co.uk

Energy

Battery rechargers
www.battery-chargers.com
www.global-batteries.co.uk

Calculate your energy costs
*For information on calculating your electricity
consumption in watts:* www.diykyoto.com

Energy-saving gadgets
Eco kettle www.greenshop.co.uk,
www.nigelsecostore.com
SAVAplug (saves 20% on running costs when fitted
to fridges and freezers) www.savawatt.com
Solar garden lights
www.naturalresourcegroup.co.uk
Wind-up torches www.freeplayenergy.com

Energy-saving light bulbs
www.greenshop.co.uk
www.london-energy.com
www.lyco.co.uk
www.nigelsecostore.com

Green energy suppliers
Ecotricity www.ecotricity.co.uk Tel 0800 326100
Good Energy www.good-energy.co.uk
Tel 0845 4561640
Green Electricity www.greenelectricity

*For more information on electricity companies
supporting renewable energy projects:* www.foe.co.uk

Renewable energy systems
British Photovoltaic Association www.pv-uk.org.uk
British Wind Energy Association www.bwea.com
The low-carbon buildings programme
www.est.org.uk

Small wind turbines

www.good-energy.co.uk

www.provenenergy.com

Solar water heaters

For advice and information on local government grants that you may be eligible for, or to find an installer near you, ring your nearest Energy Efficiency Advice Centre on 0800 512 012 or visit www.est.org. uk/myhome. The Centre for Alternative Technology also has a free information service. Visit www.cat.org.uk/information.

For more information on small-scale renewable systems:

www.bwea.com

www.cat.org.uk

www.greenenergy.org.uk

Saving energy

For more information, visit:

www.saveenergy.co.uk

www.defra.gov.uk

Environmental issues

Campaign to slash carbon dioxide emissions by 1 billion tonnes: www.globalcool.com

Friends of the Earth

26-28 Underwood Street

London N1 7JQ

www.foe.co.uk

Tel 020 7490 1555

Soil Association

South Plaza, Marlborough Street

Bristol BS1 3NX

info@soilassociation.org

Tel 0117 314 5000

Soil Association Scotland

18 Liberton Brae, Tower Mains

Edinburgh EH16 6AE

contact@sascotland.org

Tel 0131 666 2474

Food & Drink

Many supermarkets now stock a wide range of Fairtrade and organic products

Fairtrade

British Association of Fair Trade Shops

www.bafts.org.uk Tel 07796 050045

The Fairtrade Foundation

Room 204, 16 Baldwin's Gdns, London EC1N 7RJ

www.fairtrade.org.uk Tel 020 7405 5942

Farmers' markets

For information on farmers' markets:

Growing Communities

www.growingcommunities.org

London Farmers' Markets

www.lfm.org.uk Tel 020 7833 0338

National Farmers' Retail and Markets Association

www.farmersmarkets.net Tel 0845 4588 420

Scottish Association of Farmers' Markets

www.scottishfarmersmarkets.co.uk

Fruit & vegetable box schemes

Abel and Cole

www.abel-cole.co.uk Tel 0845 262 6262

(South-east England)

Farmaround Organic

www.farmaround.co.uk Tel 020 7627 8066

(North-west and north-east England)

Grow Wild

www.growwild.co.uk Tel 0845 226 3393

(Central Scotland)

Helen's Bay Organic Gardens

www.helensbayorganicgardens.com

Tel 028 9185 3122 *(Northorn Ireland)*

Riverford Organic Vegetables Ltd

www.riverford.co.uk Tel 0845 600 2311

(South England)

Fungi

For information on foraging for fungi, visit:

www.britmycolsoc.org.uk

Online fish suppliers

Deverill Trout Farm www.purelyorganic.co.uk

Graig Farm Organics www.graigfarm.co.uk

Inverawe Smokehouses www.smokedsalmon.co.uk

Loch Fyne www.lochfyne.com

The Organic Smokehouse

www.organicsmokehouse.com

Online fresh meat suppliers

Daylesford Organic www.daylesfordorganic.com

Graig Farm Organics www.graigfarm.co.uk

Helen Browning Organics

www.helenbrowningorganics.co.uk

Higher Hacknell Farm www.higherhacknell.co.uk

Sheepdrove Organic Farm www.sheepdrove.com

Well Hung Meat www.wellhungmeat.com

Organic drinks

Clipper Teas www.clipper-teas.com

Pitfield Beer Shop www.pitfieldbeershop.co.uk

Rocks organic cordials www.rocksorganic.com

Vinceremos www.vinceremos.co.uk

Vintage Roots www.vintageroots.co.uk

Garden

Apple trees in pots

Keepers Nursery www.keepers-nursery.co.uk

Tel 01622 726465

www.realenglishfruit.co.uk

Barbecue products

For locally sourced charcoal:

www.bioregional.com

Composting

Garden Organic www.gardenorganic.org.uk

Community Compost Network

www.communitycompost.org

The Composting Association www.compost.org.uk

www.wasteonline.org.uk

Green Christmas trees

The British Christmas Tree Growers Association

www.christmastree.org.uk

Living Christmas Trees

www.livingchristmastrees.co.uk

Growing vegetables
Garden Organic www.gardenorganic.org.uk

Herbs
Herb Society UK www.herbsociety.co.uk

Orchards
Brogdale Horticultural Trust www.brogdale.org
Tel 01795 535286
Bernwode Plants www.bernwodeplants.co.uk
Common Ground www.commonground.org.uk
Tel 01747 850820
Deacon's Nursery www.deaconsnurseryfruits.co.uk
Keepers Nursery www.keepers-nursery.co.uk
www.naturalengland.org.uk

Pesticide-free gardening
Garden Organic www.gardenorganic.org.uk
Pan UK www.pan-uk.org   Tel 020 7065 0905
The Royal Society for the Protection of Birds
www.rspb.org.uk

To order nematodes:
www.defenders.co.uk
www.greengardener.co.uk
www.just-green.com
www.organiccatalogue.com

Planting by the moon
Biodynamic Gardening www.peagreenboat.co.uk
www.moongardening.cwc.net
www.plantingbythemoon.co.uk

Soil care
Garden Organic www.gardenorganic.org.uk

Salad leaf seed mixes
The Organic Catalogue www.organiccatalogue.com

Wormeries & composting units
Wiggly Wigglers www.wigglywigglers.co.uk
The Green Shop www.greenshop.co.uk

Home

Bedlinen & towels
Albatross www.albatross-global.com
Tel 08708 502098
Green Fibres www.greenfibres.co.uk

Cleaning products
Baileys' products www.baileyshomeandgarden.com
Tel 01989 561931
BioCare products Tel 01628 524470
Ecover products www.ecover.com   Tel 01273 206 997
Natural Eco trading Ltd www.greenbrands.co.uk
Tel 01892 616 871
Marks & Spencer www.marksandspencer.com
The Green Shop www.greenshop.co.uk

Clothes & shoes
Clothes
Adili www.adili.com
Howies www.howies.co.uk
Inbi Hemp www.inbi-hemp.co.uk
Natural Collection www.naturalcollection.com
Pakucho www.pakucho.co.uk
People Tree www.ptree.co.uk
Schmidt Natural Clothing www.naturalclothing.co.uk
Seasalt www.seasaltorganic.co.uk

Terramar www.terramar.co.uk

The Green Apple www.the-green-apple.co.uk

Shoes

Beyond Skin www.beyondskin.co.uk

Fair Deal Trading www.fairdealtrading.co.uk

Freerangers www.freerangers.co.uk

Housing materials

Ecoconstruct www.constructionresources.com
Tel 020 7450 2211

Ecospaints www.ecospaints.com Tel 01524 852371

Eco Solutions Ltd www.ecosolutions.co.uk
Tel 01934 844 484

Green Building Store www.greenbuildingstore.co.uk
Tel 01484 854898

Presents

Ecotopia www.ecotopia.co.uk

Oxfam Unwrapped www.oxfamunwrapped.com

Good Gifts www.goodgifts.org

Reclaimed, recycled, & eco- friendly furniture & home accessories

Biome Lifestyle www.biomelifestyle.com

The Natural Collection www.naturalcollection.com

Old Ginger www.oldginger.com

Roche Bobois www.roche-bobois.com

Nigel's Eco Store www.nigelsecostore.co.uk

Milagros www.milagros.co.uk Tel 0117 983 6699

Refound Objects www.refoundobjects.com
Tel. 01434 634567

Smile Plastics www.smileplastics.co.uk
Tel 01743 850267

Personal Care

Dr.Hauschka Skin Care www.drhauschka.co.uk
Tel 01386 791 022

Lavera Organic & Natural Bodycare Products
www.lavera.co.uk Tel 01557 870 203

Natracare tampons www.natracare.com

Neal's Yard Remedies www.nealsyardremedies.com

NHR Organic Oils www.nhr.kz Tel 0845 310 8066

Organic Botanics www.organicbotanics.com
Tel 01273 773 182

REN Skincare www.renskincare.com
Tel 020 7724 2900

The Green People Company www.greenpeople.co.uk
Tel 01444 401444

The Spirit of Nature www.spiritofnature
Tel 0870 725 9885

Weleda Natural Bodycare www.weleda.co.uk
Tel 0115 944 8200

For more information on toiletries & cosmetics, visit:
Women's Environmental Network www.wen.org.uk

Livestock

Bees

There are no regulations on keeping bees in the UK. If your bees have varroa or American or European Foul Brood diseases, contact your local Inspector from the National Bee Unit.

British Beekeepers' Association

The National Beekeeping Centre
Stoneleigh Park, Warwickshire CV8 2LG
www.bbka.org.uk Tel 02476 696679

National Bee Unit
Central Science Laboratory,
Sand Hutton, York YO41 1LZ
www.nationalbeeunit.com Tel 01904 462 510

Chickens
Regulations: there are no regulations on keeping flocks of fewer than 250 birds. Contact your local Environmental Health Officer for any local bylaws.

Poultry Club of Great Britain
South Lodge, Creeton Road
Swinstead, Grantham, Lincolnshire NG33 4PG
www.poultryclub.org Tel 01476 550067

Soil Association www.soilassociation.org
Tel 0117 314 5000

The Domestic Fowl Trust
Station Road, Honeybourne, Near Evesham
Worcestershire WR11 7QZ
www.domesticfowltrust.co.uk Tel 01386 833083

Cows
Regulations on keeping of cattle are issued by Defra
(Department of Environment, Farming And Rural Affairs). *You need to obtain a County Parish Holding number from your local Rural Development Office, keep an Animal Medicine Record Book and complete an Animal Movement Licence when you move cattle.*

Defra
Customer Contact Unit, Eastbury House
30-34 Albert Embankment, London SE1 7TL
www.defra.gov.uk Tel 08459 33 55 77

Rare Breeds Survival Trust
Stoneleigh Park, Nr Kenilworth, Warwickshire
CV8 2LG www.rbst.org.uk Tel 024 7669 6551

Royal College of Veterinary Surgeons
Belgravia House, 62-64 Horseferry Road
London SW1P 2AF
www.rcvs.org.uk Tel 0207 222 2001

Soil Association www.soilassociation.org
Tel 0117 314 5000

The British Cattle Veterinary Association
The Green, Frampton-On-Severn
Gloucestershire GL2 7EP
www.bcva.org.uk Tel 01452 740816

Ducks
There are no regulations on keeping ducks. Contact your local Environmental Health Officer for any local bylaws. Ensure your duck pond does not abstract large amounts of water or produce effluent.

Poultry Club of Great Britain www.poultryclub.org
Tel 01476 550067

Soil Association www.soilassociation.org
Tel 0117 314 5000

The British Waterfowl Association
PO Box 163, Oxted RH8 0WP
www.waterfowl.org.uk Tel 01892 740212

The Domestic Fowl Trust
www.domesticfowltrust.co.uk Tel 01386 833083

Geese

There are no regulations on keeping geese. Contact your local Environmental Health Officer to check for any local bylaws.

Poultry Club of Great Britain
www.poultryclub.org Tel 01476 550067

The British Waterfowl Association
www.waterfowl.org.uk Tel 01892 740212

The Domestic Fowl Trust www.poultryclub.org
Tel 01386 833083

Soil Association www.soilassociation.org
Tel 0117 314 5000

Goats

Regulations: goats are covered by animal welfare regulations. Contact Defra for more details.

Defra www.defra.gov.uk Tel 08459 33 55 77

The British Goat Society
34-36 Fore Street Bovey Tracey
Nr Newton Abbot, Devon TQ13 9AD
www.allgoats.com Tel 01626 83316

The Goat Veterinary Society
29 Winfield, Newent, Gloucestershire GL18 1QB
www.goatvetsoc.co.uk Tel 01531 820074

Pigs

Regulations are issued by Defra (Department of Environment, Farming And Rural Affairs). You need to obtain a County Parish Holding number from your local Rural Development Office, keep an Animal Medicine Record Book and complete an Animal Movement Licence when you move pigs. If you sell a rare breed, you must join the British Pig Association. You cannot slaughter pigs on your own premises; you must take them to an approved abbatoir.

Defra www.defra.gov.uk Tel 08459 33 55 77

Pig Veterinary Society
c/o The Veterinary Laboratories Agency, West House Station Road, Thirsk, North Yorkshire YO7 1PZ
www.pigvetsoc.org.uk

Royal College of Veterinary Surgeons
www.rcvs.org.uk Tel 0207 222 2001

Rare Breeds Survival Trust www.rbst.org.uk
Tel 024 7669 6551

Soil Association www.soilassociation.org
Tel 0117 314 5000

The British Pig Association
Trumpington Mews, 40b High Street, Trumpington
Cambridge CB2 2LS
www.britishpigs.org.uk Tel 01223 845100

Recycling

Aluminium
Alupro www.alupro.org.uk Tel 0845 722 7722

Batteries
British Battery Manufacturers Association
Tel 020 7838 4878
Computers
Bytes Twice Tel 0113 243 8777
To recycle plastics:
www.recoup.org

For more information on the different ways you can recycle your rubbish, visit:
The Recycle Works www.recycleworks.co.uk
Wastewatch www.wastewatch.org.uk
Community Recycling Network www.crn.org.uk

Transport

Carbon footprint
Carbon Trust www.thecarbontrust.co.uk
Tel 020 7170 7000
To calculate the carbon emissions you create, visit:
www.myfootprint.org

Car-sharing schemes
www.liftshare.org

Cycle routes & cycling campaigns
www.lcc.org.uk
www.sustrans.org

Electric cars & scooters
Electric Car Association www.avt.uk.com
Tel 0182 348 0196
Scoot Electric www.scootelectric.co.uk
Tel 08707 877 408

Hybrid cars & scooters
For information on eco-friendly transport, visit:
www.eta.co.uk

Water

Toilet water-saver devices
Hippo Water Saver www.hippo-the-watersaver.co.uk
For low-flush toilets and water-saving showerheads:
Bathstore.com www.bathstore.com
Tel 020 8773 5000

Wildlife

Garden wildlife
British Hedgehog Preservation Society
www.britishhedgehogs.org.uk
Bug Life www.buglife.org.uk
English Nature www.english-nature.org.uk

Plants to help wildlife
Garden Organic www.gardenorganic.org.uk
The Royal Society for the Protection of Birds
www.rspb.org.uk
Wild About Gardens www.wildaboutgardens.co.uk

Wildlife ponds
Centre for Ecology and Hydrology www.ceh.ac.uk
English Nature www.english-nature.org.uk
Garden Organic www.gardenorganic.org.uk
Pond Conservation www.pondstrust.org.uk

INDEX

Page numbers in italics indicate a boxed entry. Entries in italics indicate a recipe or a Latin plant name. Latin names are not given for vegetables, fruit and herbs.

tomatoes for 72–3
harvesting
fruit 276–9
honey *265*
hawthorn 145
heat pumps 211
heating
heating water naturally 194–5
wood-burning stove 226–7
Hedera see ivies
hedgehogs 161, 321
hedges for wildlife 248
herbs 149
aromatic 272
in containers 28–31, 170–1
decorative 272
designing a herb garden 270–5
drying 46–7
flea collar *70*
growing tips 273
herb mash 80
for kitchen 272
repelling insects *257*
teas and infusions 168–71
wild 60–3
hive, making 263–4
holidays, green issues *76*
honey 119, 260–5
harvesting *265*
hops *63*
household appliances, energy-saving 22
household items, reusing 52
hoverflies 161
humus *200*
hydro power 211
hyssop *170–1*

I

Iberis see candytuft
infusions, herb 168–71
insecticides
in fabrics *95*
plant-based *160*
insects
attracting *144*, 160–1, 244–9, 257, 321
pondlife 326
repelling 254–7
insulation 22
Irish coffee 293
ivies 145

J

Jack-by-the-hedge *62*
jams 234, 242–3
Jerusalem artichokes *209*
juicing 202–3

K

kettles as gifts, eco-friendly 93
kitchen waste 129

L

label checking 24, 48–9
lacewings 161
ladybirds 161
lamb's lettuce *see* corn salad
land cress 21
lavender *170–1*
leafhoppers 254, 257
leaflets for campaigning 86–7
leafmould 200
legumes 149, 208, *209*
providing nutrients 257
lemon balm *170–1*
lemonade, mint 293
lemons, storing *279*
letters for campaigning 86–7, *87*
lettuces *148*, 149, 208
summer varieties *21*
in windowboxes 20
lifestyle changes 8–15
light bulbs, energy-saving 22, 23
limescale remover 49
Limnanthes see poached egg plant
linens, organic, as gifts 92
linoleum 134
liqueur as gifts, homemade 93
local businesses, supporting 42–3
loft insulation 22
log piles for wildlife 318
lollies 250–1
lunar calendars 324

M

Macrolepiota rhacodes see Shaggy parasol
Malus see apple trees; crab apple trees
manures, green 198
marigolds 257, *258*
marjoram
in containers 28
wild 31
MDF *see* fibreboard, medium density
metal, recycling 52, 53
metal polish 49
methane 128
mice *70*
microfibre cleaning cloths 45
micro-generation schemes 210–11
milk
cow's *284*
goat's 304–6
milk paint *132*
mineral bath 35
mint *31*, 257, 273
mint lemonade 293
mizuna 20, *21*
moon, planting by 324–5
mosquitoes *69*
moth control *69*, 70
muffins, blueberry 123
mulching 155, *196*, 198, 217
mulled wine 293
mushrooms *see* fungi
mustard 257
oriental, summer varieties *21*

N

nappies, natural 58–9
as gifts 93
nappy rash 59
nasturtiums 257, 258
nasturtium vinegar 38
nectar providers 249
nectarines 125
nematodes 161
nesting sites for birds 320
nettles *62*
newts 161, 249
nutrients for vegetables 257

O

oak trees 249
oils
flavoured 36–7
for skin care *33, 83*
olives: *red pepper and olive scones* 79
onions 208, *209*
as companion plants 257, *258*
orchards 212–19
harvesting fruit 276–9
organic products
bath products *35*
drinks 290–3
fabrics 94–7
fertilizers 198–9
foods 24–6, 42
organic gardening 254
vegetable growing *147*
skin care products 64–5
oven cleaner *49*

P

paints 132–3
paper, recycling 52, 53
parasol fungus 102
parsley 31
in containers 28
providing nutrients 257
repelling insects 257
parsnip soup with ginger 81
peaches 125
freezing 233
pears 125
apple, pear and ginger juice 202
freezing 233
harvesting 276
orchards 214–15
preserving 235
peat-free compost advantages *121*
peppermint *170–1*
infusion 168
perfumed products *85*
pest controls 68–71
pesticides 24–6, 26
avoiding 160–1
used on cotton crops 95
petitions for campaigning 86–7
Phacelia tanacetifolia as green manure
198

ACKNOWLEDGMENTS

The publisher would like to thank the following for their kind permission to reproduce their photographs:
(a-above; b-below/bottom; c-centre; f-far; l-left; r-right; t-top)
9 Anthony Blake Photo Library: Ming Tang Evans. **21 GAP Photos Ltd:** John Glover (tr); Maddie Thornhill (tl) (cb). **Garden World Images:** T. McGlinchey (br). **62 Alamy Images:** Pat Tuson (br). **FLPA:** Nigel Cattlin (cl) (cr); Foto Natura Stock (c); Tony Wharton (bc). **63 FLPA:** Nigel Cattlin (cr) (cl). Garden Picture Library: David Cavagnaro (bl). Garden World Images: H. Harrison (bc). **73 Garden Picture Library:** Friedrich Strauss (l). **77 Alamy Images:** Stephen Vowles. **120 Garden World Images:** F. Davis. **125 Andrew Lawson. 129** www.wigglywigglers.co.uk. **136 Nicola Browne:** Designer: Isabelle Greene. **146 GAP Photos Ltd:** John Glover/Design: Land Art, Hampton Court Flower Show 2000. **149 DK Images:** Jacqui Hurst (bc). **156 Modeste Herwig. 158 GAP Photos Ltd:** John Glover (cr); Juliette Wade (bc). **Garden World Images:** (bl) & A. Graham (br); **The Garden Collection:** Torie Chugg (tc). **Garden Picture Library:** John Glover (cl). **Garden Exposures Photo Library:** Andrea Jones (tl). **Clive Nichols:** (c). **Courtesy of Thompson & Morgan** (tr). **164 Clive Nichols:** Vale End, Surrey. **184 John Tarren/David Scrivener Archive. 185 John Tarren/David Scrivener Archive** (tr) (c) & (br). **218 GAP Photos Ltd:** Paul Debois (bc) (br). **Garden Picture Library:** Howard Rice (bl). **The Garden Collection:** Derek St Romaine (cr). **226 Garden Picture Library. 227 Courtesy of Jotul As. 230** Cut flower statistics supplied by The *Ecologist*. **239 John Tarren/** **David Scrivener Archive. 241 Eye Ubiquitous:** G Redmayne (tl). **259 Garden Picture Library:** Botanica (bl). **261 Marianne Majerus Photography:** Designer: Stephen Crisp. **277 Corbis:** O'Brien Productions. **281 Corbis:** Robert Dowling (br). **295 John Tarren/David Scrivener Archive. 306 Ardea:** Kenneth W. Fink (tl). **FLPA:** Foto Natura Stock (tr). **307 Corbis:** James Marshall (tl). **FLPA:** R P Lawrence (tc). **OSF:** Gary Griffen (tr). **314 Alamy Images:** Alex Hess (clb). **Cephas Picture Library:** Peter Barr (cla); John Davies (bl). **Modeste Herwig:** (bc). **Ken Muir Ltd:** (tl). **Fred Lyon:** (ca). **Courtesy of Flag Hill Winery & Distillery, Lee, New Hampshire, USA:** (crb). **Photos Horticultural:** (tr). **334 ArdeaLondon** (bl). **Courtesy of British Pig Executive** (fbr). **Corbis:** Robert Dowling (bc). **DK Images:** Weald and Downland Open Air Museum, Chichester (cl). **Ecoscene:** Frank Blackburn (tr). **FLPA:** Sarah Rowland (c)

DK would like to thank the following people for help with location photographs:
Daphne Lambert of Penrhos Court, Kington (food); Jane Howard (smallholding livestock and bees); Saskia Marjoram (cut flowers); Ticklemore Cheese, Totnes; James & Karen Skevington (ducks and geese).

Sheherazade Goldsmith would like to thank: Annie Gatti, Erica Bower, Daphne Lambert, Matilda Lee, Pat Thomas and Robert Yarham; everyone at DK who worked on the book; The *Ecologist*; Richard and Kirsty; and my husband, Zac.